D0595214

THE ARAB
WORLD

GERALD BUTT

THE ARAB WORLD

Foreword by

PETER MANSFIELD

The Dorsey Press

Chicago, Illinois 60604

Cover
Front cover TOP Frank Spooner Pictures; CENTRE The Image Bank/Jay Freis; BOTTOM Frank Spooner Pictures   **Back cover** Frank Spooner Pictures

Section one
Page i TOP Alan Wilding; BOTTOM LEFT Frank Spooner Pictures; BOTTOM RIGHT Frank Spooner Pictures   **Page ii** Gerald Butt   **Page iii** TOP Gerald Butt; BOTTOM LEFT Gerald Butt; BOTTOM RIGHT Alan Wilding   **Page iv** TOP Alan Wilding; BOTTOM Gerald Butt   **Page v** TOP Alan Wilding; BOTTOM Gerald Butt   **Page vi** TOP Egyptian State Tourist Office; BOTTOM Frank Spooner Pictures   **Page vii** TOP LEFT Frank Spooner Pictures; TOP RIGHT Frank Spooner Pictures; BOTTOM The Photo Source   **Page viii** Tunisian National Tourist Board

Section two
Page ix TOP Frank Spooner Pictures; BOTTOM Frank Spooner Pictures   **Page x** Frank Spooner Pictures   **Page xi** TOP Frank Spooner Pictures; BOTTOM Frank Spooner Pictures   **Page xii** TOP United Arab Emirates Embassy; BOTTOM United Arab Emirates Embassy   **Page xiii** TOP LEFT Alan Wilding; TOP RIGHT United Arab Emirates Embassy; BOTTOM Frank Spooner Pictures   **Page xiv** TOP Frank Spooner Pictures; BOTTOM The Photo Source   **Page xv** TOP Frank Spooner Pictures; BOTTOM Frank Spooner Pictures   **Page xvi** TOP Moroccan National Tourist Office; BOTTOM Rex Features Ltd

First published in 1987 by BBC Enterprises Ltd
Published in 1988 by
The Dorsey Press,
224 South Michigan Avenue,
Suite 440, Chicago,
Illinois 60604

ISBN 0-256-06100-9
Library of Congress Number 87-70522

2 3 4 5 6 7 8 ML 3 2 1 0 9 8

Typeset in 11/13 Linotron Palatino by Phoenix Photosetting, Chatham
Printed and bound in England by Mackays of Chatham Ltd, Kent
Cover printed by White Quill Press, Surrey

Contents

Foreword   6

1 The Arabs   9
   A shared language, a common culture

2 Islam   22
   Unity and division

3 Egypt   33
   The heart-beat of the Arab world

4 Lebanon   45
   The devastated country

5 The Palestinians   67
   A people in search of a home

6 Jordan and Syria   81
   A kingdom looking West, a republic looking East

7 The Gulf States   97
   Ancient traditions, modern wealth

8 The Gulf War   115
   A forgotten conflict

9 The Maghreb   124
   Lands of the west

10 Sudan and the Yemens   144
   At the borders of the Arab world

Index   150

Foreword

All peoples are shaped by their history but none more so than the Arabs. They combine a vibrant sense of their inheritance from a golden past of a great Arab/Islamic civilisation with a gnawing awareness of the subsequent humiliating triumph of an arrogant West. Thus while there are certain constant and unchanging elements in the Arab world – of which the Holy Koran is the supreme example – there is turbulence on the surface. The pace of history has enormously accelerated in the past century, a brief period in the life of an ancient people. Well into this century the colonial powers of Europe began to devour and then destroyed the Muslim Ottoman Empire which had provided a stable framework for the Arab world for four centuries. Within three decades the old imperialisms were replaced by the two new superpowers, more distant but no less dominant. The septic wound of Palestine remained to poison the Arab body. These events coincided with the discovery that the most fiercely conservative of the Arabs possessed an enormous share of the energy needs of the industrialised world. They had to find ways of absorbing the sudden wealth this brought without destroying their ancient values and identity. Having done this with considerable success they now find themselves faced with an equally sudden and enormous drop in income. In these circumstances some degree of national neurosis is to be expected.

Faced with the complex, conflicting and sometimes apparently incomprehensible passions of the Arab world, some Westerners prefer to abandon all effort at understanding, taking refuge in a cliché image of the Arabs as terrorists or spendthrifts. But this is unwise as well as hypocritical in view of our share of responsibility for their present situation. At least for West Europeans, the Arabs will remain our nearest neighbours, with countless common interests. The continuation of a Euro-Arab dialogue is not only politic but essential.

It seems to me that in this short book Gerald Butt has made a valuable contribution to the dialogue. He starts off with the natural advantage of a childhood spent among Arabs when his father was stationed in Jordan and the Gulf. This not only provides him with memories which make illuminating asides, but helps him to explain the apparent paradox of a Middle East which is both constant and changing. Thirty years ago the Western powers still regarded the Arab world as a satellite region – comparable to the US view of Central America as its own backyard. The Suez War, which destroyed most of the pretensions of the old colonial powers, was still to come. The independence of what was still French North Africa also lay ahead, as did Britain's final withdrawal from the fringes of Arabia. For Englishmen under forty it is hard to imagine what the Middle East was like in the 1950s but Gerald Butt can draw on his own childhood recollections to help him.

It is of great importance that his feeling for the region enables him to make such good use of his more recent experiences. Every one of the Western reporters who has endured the risks of reporting from Lebanon during the endless civil war and invasion deserves the highest praise for courage. Not all have been equally successful at giving meaning to these events. A book of this kind inevitably has to be impressionistic, but without a solid substructure of knowledge it would be useless. This knowledge is essential before one can even begin to explain either the conflicting passions which are destroying Lebanon or the apparently mindless slaughter of the Gulf War. Historical understanding is needed, too, in order to interpret less violent but no less mysterious phenomena, such as the differences between the Arabs of the East or Mashrek, who to the British are, for historical reasons, 'typical', and those of North Africa or the Maghreb, who are an equal component of the Arab world and at least as important in the Euro-Arab dialogue.

There is one aspect of prime importance on which no final judgement can be made and Gerald Butt wisely refrains from making any. This is the relative strength of the militant Islamic movements (to avoid the term 'fundamentalism' which can be misleading) and other popular forces such as Arab nationalism or – a phenomenon which is too often ignored – the territorial nationalism which has gathered around the flags of the Arab nation states. Because the boundaries of these states were largely artificial and devised by westerners, the Arabs assumed that no such nationalisms would arise. Time has shown this to be false. Iraqi, Syrian, Jordanian or Algerian nationalism are recognisable forces in Arab politics.

Is there a future for Islamic Utopianism among the Arabs? By this

I mean the belief that all they have to do is to install true Islamic governments, applying only the Holy Shari'a or God's law, and all their humiliations and divisions and besetting social problems will be removed. Has this Utopianism been helped or hindered by the Khomeini factor, which is suspect to most Arabs because it is both Iranian and Shiite, but which has demonstrably established Islamic government of a kind and defers less to either superpower than any Arab regime? In the admirable chapter on Islam the author has suggested some points for consideration. I would only raise a small doubt about his apparent acceptance of the common assumption that 'secular Arab nationalism' identified with Nasser has died. In the first place Arab nationalism can never really be secular because of the wide overlap between Arabism and Islam. Nasser understood this, as do the present rulers of Saudi Arabia who champion both. Secondly, the Arab Baathist ideology, which is close to Nasserism in many respects, is still dominant in Syria and Iraq. It may be swept aside by Islamic militancy but this has yet to happen.

Good reporting of the Arab world requires both a firm grasp of the historical background and a real understanding of the emotions which sway the Arab soul. Gerald Butt clearly has both these qualities. He would never claim to be answering all the questions about the Arabs, but with a combination of sympathy and cool analysis he offers a vivid and informative introduction to the contemporary Arab world.

Peter Mansfield
February 1987

1 The Arabs

A shared language, a common culture

The connotations of the word 'Arab' in the English language are numerous. They relate to the various stereotype visions fixed in Western minds as to who the Arabs are, what their life-style is like and where they live. In common use are terms such as 'street Arab' (the notion that all Arabs are cunning, unwashed beggars), 'oil-rich sheikh' (the notion that all Arabs have made fortunes from oil, have a Rolls for every member of the family, and are now intent on buying up the most favourable property in London) and 'thieving Arab' (the notion that all Arabs are, by nature, untrustworthy liars and cheats). If all the various epithets that have been in use from time to time are looked at closely, it is not hard to see that the Arabs have had a pretty raw deal at the hands of the English language.

And then there's the general impression, which has inevitably gained ground over recent years, that the word 'Arab' is inter-changeable with 'terrorist'. If one gets one's news from headlines, then this is hardly surprising. Crude and obscene acts of terror carried out by extremist Palestinians and others (for reasons which I'll be examining later) have been making the front pages for years, providing fuel both to those who want to discredit the Arab cause and to those already steeped in prejudice.

In contrast – though equally erroneous – there's the romantic view of the Arabs, a view perhaps less popular these days than in the past, but still alive. It's the rosy vision of the desert sheikh (pro-nounced 'sheek' in Hollywood) portrayed in musicals like *The Desert Song*, riding his camel and living in tents, or carrying the dark-eyed, yashmaked heroine off into the sands, with the promise of a thousand delights in store. The premise of books, musicals and plays of this kind is that the Arab world consists of open deserts jewelled with oases, peopled by handsome princes and filled with Aladdin's caves where tales of the *1001 Nights* are enacted against a backdrop of beautiful women from the harem.

The more recent public images of the Arabs have been related in some way or other to oil. The big rise in oil prices in the mid-1970s prompted many Arabs to come to Europe to invest and spend their money, and prompted even larger numbers of foreigners to head for the Gulf states in search of their fortunes. Hence the newer image of the Arabs lazing around in Europe, drinking and gambling while their mini-states back home were run on their behalf by armies of foreign labour. And as the foreign firms scrambled greedily for the very considerable fortunes to be made in the Middle East at that time, so the basic ignorance about the area surfaced. I remember seeing an advertisement in London during that era which was trying to sell an Arabic language course. The gist of the advertisement was: if this scribble (Arabic writing) means nothing to you, you should sign up for our course. In fact, some of the letters in the sample sentence had been written upside down. It just didn't matter in that frantic grab for money.

It would be wrong to say that there is absolutely no foundation of truth in most of these popular images of the Arabs. Like all peoples they have their faults and the purpose of this book is most certainly not to whitewash them. Rather, the intention is to make one very basic point: the Arab world is a very varied region, steeped in history and with a rich cultural heritage, containing people who often differ considerably in outlook. They live in contrasting geographical and economic conditions. In appearance they vary from deep black to fair-skinned. In short, the term covers such a wealth of variety that there is no typical Arab, any more than there is a typical European or African.

And really how could there be? There are reckoned to be some 175–200 million Arabs in the world living in more than twenty Arab countries. It is a vast region stretching from the Atlantic Ocean in the west and encompassing the southern and eastern shores of the Mediterranean. In area, Saudi Arabia alone is larger than the whole of Western Europe. So are Algeria and Sudan.

For sure there's plenty of desert, there are plenty of palm trees, and there are still camels to be found if you're in search of what undoubtedly remains the most popular picture-postcard image of what the Arab world looks like. For sure too there are plenty of mosques and plenty of oil wells. But there's a lot more besides. And if I'm asked to say what immediately comes to mind when the words 'Arab World' are spoken, I have to admit to no single fixed image. Rather there is a collage of fragments of memory: the smell and congestion of Cairo in mid-summer; the breath-taking beauty of the snow-covered mountains in Lebanon; the coral reefs below the shallow waters of the Gulf; the endless and featureless tracts of desert in the Sahara; the Atlantic breakers crashing onto the coast of Morocco; the early morning mist rolling up the Jordan valley from the Dead Sea; the pale pink light which caresses the stone buildings of Jerusalem; the nightmare memory of a Beirut car-bomb and the sight of a man carrying his dead baby aloft, its limbs flopping like those of a rag doll; the excavators digging a mass grave in a village in southern Lebanon after an Israeli raid and a child, standing apart from the crowd of mourners, weeping hysterically; the overwhelming hospitality of a Christian family in Lebanon who invited me to share their Easter with them; the rain-sodden streets of Tunis in winter; the unbearable humidity of Bahrain in August; the amazing remnants of ancient civilisations; and so on for hours. A kaleidoscope – always variety, always change.

Europeans, and Britons in particular, have for centuries been drawn to the Arab world. In part the attraction sprang from economic and military needs, the Middle East, with the Suez Canal, lying on the route to India. In part too, though, a number of Britons became genuinely fascinated by the Arabs as people. Orientalism in the broadest sense became a matter for serious study. The British public generally became fascinated by the subject too, so that a figure like T. E. Lawrence ('Lawrence of Arabia') became a legend in his own lifetime. And as the European orientalists spread their views of what the Arabs were like, the politicians began – in the years after the Second World War – carving up the Middle East in a way that suited their interests. As we will see later, their actions set the stage for much of the violence and political wranglings that are being acted out today.

The Arab world began taking shape in the seventh century, with the birth of Islam in Mecca. From the heart of their 'Arabian' peninsula (what is now Saudi Arabia) the Arab armies headed out far and wide – north across the lands at the eastern end of the Mediterranean and west across the peninsula that joins Africa to Asia, Sinai. As they went they defeated and brought the new religion to the Persians, the Egyptians and the Berbers of North Africa. The new empire quickly assimilated local populations and local customs within the umbrella of Islam. It was inevitable, therefore, that the outlook and temperament of, for example, an Arabised Berber was going to be different from those of a bedouin of the Arabian peninsula or a sophisticated scholar from Baghdad.

These kinds of differences and variations are still in evidence

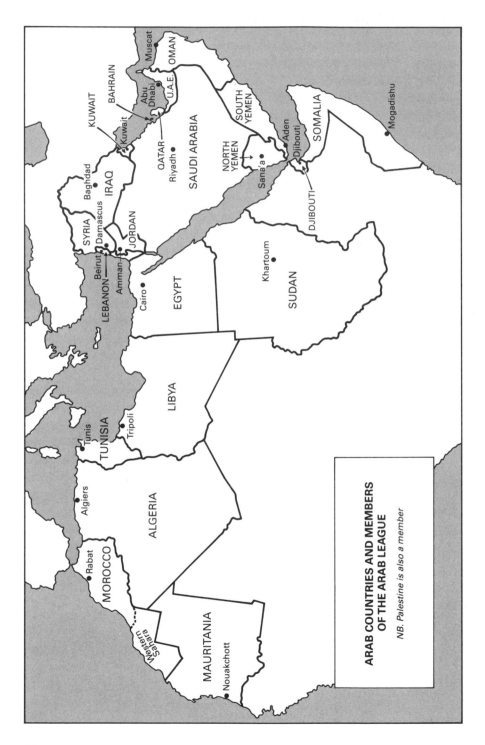

ARAB COUNTRIES AND MEMBERS
OF THE ARAB LEAGUE

NB. Palestine is also a member

today. In fact, given the size of the Arab world, it is perhaps a wonder that there is any cohesion linking the coppersmith living in the ancient walled city of Fez in Morocco with the fisherman from Bahrain in the Gulf or with the businessman from Saudi Arabia. So, what does it mean to be 'Arab'? Definitions have flowed from the pens of Western writers over the years, but seldom from the mouths of Arabs themselves. It's a question I have put to many Arabs. Two answers in particular seemed to point to a definition.

The first comes from a Muslim from Morocco, a university professor: 'Historically the Arabs were never a pure race. The only link is not, as many Europeans think, religious, but cultural. You know, even the Christian Arabs who might be against anything Islamic in the Arab culture still consider themselves as Arabs – and sometimes they are more Arab than the Arab Muslims. I had the same experience in California in the United States with families who had emigrated to America at the beginning of this century. They no longer have any direct link with the Arab community, but for purely cultural reasons still feel themselves as Arabs. I would say that Arabism is essentially the language and the culture. You can be of Berber origin, Jewish origin, African origin or European origin. But if you participate in any way in the Arab culture, you are an Arab.'

The second answer comes from a young Lebanese lady, a Christian living in a Muslim area: 'I do feel a certain solidarity with Arabs from other countries because we speak the same language. When you attend an international conference, for example, and you meet people speaking Arabic you automatically want to be with them. I don't know, maybe it's the magic of the language. Culturally there's a certain Arab unity, but politically each regime has decided otherwise. I think that what happens on the upper levels of society has little to do with the lower levels. Being an Arab, on the one hand you feel proud because you come from a culture which has given a lot to the West in the Middle Ages and has participated in building the world civilisation. On the other hand, you are fighting prejudice because of the political situation in the Arab world. Lots of people only see Arabs as terrorists, or as violent or emotional.'

That stress on culture and the reference to what the Arabs have given to the West may cause some surprise. For I know from my own experience that a good many people in Europe and the United States have no idea that there is such a thing as Arab culture, let alone that Western science and culture are indebted to the Arabs. I recall telling a fellow graduate at university that my course included Arabic language and literature. 'Is there any Arab literature?' he asked in all seriousness.

The golden era of Arab learning was roughly in the period from the eighth to the twelfth century, when the Arab world stretched almost to India in the east and up through Spain almost to Paris in the west (the Arab armies did in fact reach Poitiers before being defeated in 732). Even before the birth of Islam, though, Arabic poetry flourished in the Arabian peninsula. Not unnaturally, much of the imagery was taken from the desert, but the themes were frequently of love and sexual attraction. Around the time of the Prophet Muhammad a poet called Majnun Laila (literally meaning 'mad about Laila', so-called because of his infatuation with this lady) was writing these lines:

When Laila was a small tomboy her friends
Could see no bumps on her blouse. I loved her.
As children we were shepherds of the flock:
I wish the lambs, and ourselves, had never moved.

(Translated by George Wightman and Abdullah al-Udhari)

The expansion of the Arab Empire brought Arab scholars into contact with other cultures. They were soon translating Greek and Persian texts and developing their own schools of thought. Through Spain and Italy much of this learning passed into Europe. Trigonometry, for example, is an Arab invention; algebra is a pure Arabic word; many of the names of stars have Arab origins; the lute, the favourite instrument of the European courts in the Middle Ages, came from the Arabic 'el-oud'. A quick skim through a dictionary throws up an astonishing number of words in everyday English usage, such as alcohol and cotton, coffee and safari, which came from Arabic:

admiral	almanac	assassin	candy	drub
alchemy	amber	artichoke	cipher	muslin
alkali	arsenal	borax	divan	nadir

The gradual decaying of the golden age of the Arab Empire was hastened by external pressures. Christian armies began the slow reconquest of Spain until the Arabs were finally expelled from their last stronghold in Granada in 1492. But the Arabs left a legacy of architecture in the south of the country which can still be seen today, and a profound influence on the Spanish language. The Crusaders became the first outside European military force to stake a claim to areas of the eastern Mediterranean which were later to be the picking grounds of the European colonial powers; and the Turkish influence increased, both through the growing power of Turkish slaves and through later Turkish armed invasions. In the sixteenth century, large tracts of the Arab world, notably along the north African coast and in the countries of the eastern Mediterranean, became part of the Turkish (Ottoman) Empire. The Ottoman Empire itself was to leave a rich legacy, particularly in art and architecture, but generally this was the signal for a period of cultural and religious stagnation which lasted some 400 years until the arrival of the French and British colonial powers who eventually, after the First World War, defeated the Turks and helped bring about the downfall of their Empire.

From the 1920s on, the Arab world gradually woke from its 400 years of sleep; but it had much to catch up with. The Industrial Revolution had transformed Europe into the dominant region in the globe. The Europeans had a sophisticated culture which had seen the flowering of the novel and the play (neither existed in the Arab world at the beginning of the twentieth century) and their scientists were busy challenging the assumptions that had been accepted for centuries. This was a traumatic period for the Arabs; shedding four centuries of stagnation was no easy matter, especially when it was considered heresy to challenge the dogma of Islam to bring it into line with twentieth-century thought. As we shall see, the battle of tradition versus reform is one that has not been resolved today and it accounts in part for the differences which can still be detected between different countries and different regions. So it is, for example, that men and women in the Gulf states tend to wear traditional clothes, while the daily dress in Syria or Lebanon is, for most people, similar to the dress of European countries.

An even more interesting example can be found in the status of women in the Arab world. The assumption in the West tends to be that all Arab women live under the thumb of men; many Europeans assume that Arab women must always stay at home – indeed that they must be veiled if they appear in public and accept the status of being one among a number of wives. Like many other such generalisations this is partly true. But only partly. Wafa'

Stefan, a co-editor of a magazine published in Beirut by the Institute of Women's Studies in the Arab World, points out that, like much else in the region, the status of women reflects the laws and outlook of particular countries to the extent that they have accepted or rejected Western influence. 'For example,' she says, 'Arab countries which maintain the traditional Islamic law (as prescribed in the Koran) as the basis for the law governing personal status are countries, in general, where women are indeed under the thumb of men. But in countries where secular regimes are in power (in Syria and Iraq, for example) then women have more freedom.'

But even this is too simple a picture. To take two traditional Islamic states as an example: Kuwaiti women currently have far more freedom than Saudis and the rapidly advancing education of women throughout the Gulf amounts to something of a minor revolution. In short, Kuwaiti women today have more freedom than is the case with many secular Arabs. Then there are countries like Egypt where the law is partly traditional Islamic and partly secular, and where the two influences are regularly involved in a tug-of-war. In yet another case – Lebanon – the personal status of the individual depends more than anything else on which particular community that person happens to be part of. Young Christian women in Lebanon (until recently even those living in mainly Muslim areas) tend to enjoy relative freedom akin to that of women in the European states bordering on the Mediterranean. It is 'relative' because while they may wear the latest fashions from Paris and be seen alone at parties or night-clubs, they are still bound to their families and do not have the right to buy or sell property – which Muslim women do have.

As with other areas of Arab life, there is no absolute truth – and within all Arab countries the picture is further complicated by the difference between cities and country areas. And even if a woman seems chained to her home this doesn't mean she is devoid of power and influence. Wafa' Stefan says that in general 'women, socially, have quite a lot of power especially if they are married, and particularly if they have a son'. (My first two children were girls. The common reaction among my Arab friends was: 'Never mind, better luck next time.') Once an Arab woman has produced a son (the importance of the event is such that the father takes the title 'Abu' – 'father of' – followed by his son's name) she will have an important say in his education and on such matters as whom he should marry.

Country (Capital)	Population	Area (sq miles)	Population Density per sq mile
Algeria (Algiers)	22,000,000	920,000	24
Bahrain (Manama)	400,000	255	1570
Djibouti (Djibouti)	350,000	8,800	40
Egypt (Cairo)	46,000,000	387,000	120
Iraq (Baghdad)	15,000,000	168,000	89
Jordan (Amman)			
East Bank	2,500,000	35,000	71
West Bank	1,250,000	2,000	625
Kuwait (Kuwait)	2,000,000	7,000	285
Lebanon (Beirut)	3,500,000	4,000	875
Libya (Tripoli)	3,500,000	680,000	5
Mauritania (Nouakchott)	1,800,000	398,000	4.5
Morocco (Rabat)	23,000,000	177,000	130
Oman (Muscat)	1,500,000	105,000	14
Qatar (Doha)	260,000	4,500	58
Saudia Arabia (Riyudh)	8,500,000	927,000	9
Somalia (Mogadishu)	4,000,000	246,000	16
Sudan (Khartoum)	21,000,000	968,000	21
Syria (Damascus)	10,000,000	72,000	139
Tunisia (Tunis)	7,000,000	63,000	111
U.A.E. (Abu Dhabi)	1,200,000	32,300	37
N. Yemen/Yemen Arab Republic (Sana'a)	8,000,000	73,000	109
S. Yemen/People's Democratic Republic of Yemen (Aden)	2,000,000	111,000	18

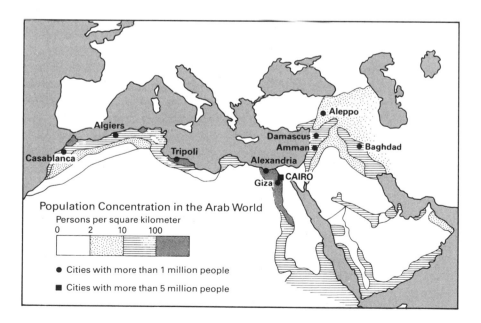

Population Concentration in the Arab World

Persons per square kilometer

0   2   10   100

● Cities with more than 1 million people

■ Cities with more than 5 million people

The question of women going out to work varies considerably from country to country too. In some countries – Lebanon, Egypt and Tunisia, for instance – it is common to see women working alongside men in offices and in other places. In Saudi Arabia a law states that there should be no mixing between the sexes whether in schools, universities or places of work. That doesn't mean that women don't get educated. They do, but they tend to move into job areas such as the medical field where their only contact will be with other women and with children. Wafa' Stefan says though that, in general, education has been for women 'the ticket for freedom'. True, there is an Islamic revival (see p. 31) and many Islamic militants would like to reverse most aspects of what we in the West regard as female liberation. But the next generations of women will have greater opportunities than the current ones, and not in spite of Islam as a whole – only of a certain type of Islam that is reactionary in the purest sense.

So the Arab world is a complex weave of variety and variation, yet it is without any doubt a unit and has many unifying factors. I have mentioned how language and culture are binding factors. Colloquial Arabic differs considerably from region to region, even from country to country. But a modern version of classical Arab (the language of the Koran), which could be termed literary Arabic, is understood throughout the whole Arab world and indeed anywhere in the world where people are familiar with the language. This formal Arabic is the language used by newsreaders and found in newspapers throughout the region. It is the language too of formal inter-Arab meetings. But while a foreigner speaking formal Arabic will be able to make himself understood, he will sound very strange indeed. Egyptian Arabic is probably the most widely understood of the national variations because it is to be heard on the sound track of Egyptian films and television soap operas, which are by far the most numerous and popular in the region.

A love of music and poetry is also shared by most Arabs. Singers like the formidable Egyptian lady, Umm Qulthoum, who died a few years ago, could move an audience to tears in any corner of the Middle East, despite her great age. Of the younger generation the Lebanese singer Fairouz has an enormous following. Her gentle, trilling, plangent voice sends shivers down my spine whenever I hear her. I remember playing a record of her singing Christmas carols in Arabic to a visiting colleague from London to demonstrate what an astonishingly moving performance she could give. He looked at me with disbelief. He couldn't understand how anyone could like Arab music. In my experience, few foreigners who live in the Middle East develop a taste for the music; apart from the language difficulty, the quarter-tone note separation grates on some Western ears.

Where a unifying force in the Arab world is most obviously missing is at the level of inter-state co-operation. The greatest single trauma that the region suffered was the creation of the Zionist state of Israel in the heart of the Arab nation. It remains today the single dominant issue for Arabs which in some way or other colours almost everything that happens in the Middle East. For the Arabs it represents the ultimate betrayal by the colonial powers, and by Britain in particular. It is the greatest source of resentment and bitterness, and is seen more than anything else as being the cause of divisions among Arab countries. One veteran Arab diplomat expressed it this way: 'Israel is the cancer in the Arab body.' The question has been asked time and time again since Israel was born in 1948: why have the Arabs, with their hugely superior numbers, and in recent years their very great oil wealth, not been able to unite sufficiently to stand up to Israel? For the truth is that since 1948, Israel's boundaries have actually been extended as a result of war. Part of the answer is that the United States is committed to supporting Israel and guaranteeing its well-being. It does this by injecting billions of dollars of aid into the country and giving it, in the view of the Arabs, unquestioned political support, regardless of the damage caused to US–Arab relations. Traditional Arab friends of the United States, like King Hussein of Jordan, feel bitter and betrayed by this.

Another part of the answer is that the Israelis have bought from the United States and developed at home armaments which are more sophisticated than those found in the Arab world. They also use their weapons with more skill than the Arabs, possibly because their motivation – that of survival – is greater.

In the end, though, one has to say that the failure of the Arabs to unite to face Israel is no different from its failure to unite over almost every issue that has arisen. The 1950s and 1960s were the years when, as one state after another threw off the yokes of colonialism, the Arabs felt they could sink their differences in a common cause. This was the era which fed on the rhetoric of secular pan-Arab unity, which, it was believed, would replace Western domination and enable the Arabs to confront Israel. It was a dream fostered above all by that giant of a country, Egypt, and in particular by that giant of a leader, President Gamal Abdel-Nasser. This era, though, came to a spectacular close in June 1967 when the Six Day War with Israel began. The humiliating defeat was a catastrophe for President Nasser, for Egypt, for the whole of the Arab world and for the hopes of pan-Arab unity. Nasser never really recovered. Pride was restored to a large extent by the next Arab-Israeli war of 1973, the aftermath of which brought euphoria to the Arab world, with the oil-producing states realising, and for a time using to their advantage, the hold they had over an oil-hungry West. But the euphoria and the unity were short-lived. Other issues split the region: Egypt's decision to sign a peace treaty with Israel, the Gulf War between Iraq and Iran, the character and policies of the Palestine Liberation Organisation (PLO), and much more. By the mid-1980s the hopes of convening an Arab summit with all heads of state present seemed to have disappeared for good.

The body which tries to co-ordinate the views and actions of the various Arab countries is the Arab League, which was formed in 1954 by the handful of states which were independent at the time. Today there are 22 members (see p. 12) made up of all the Arab states, along with Djibouti, Mauritania and Somalia. One of the League's Assistant Secretary-Generals, Mr Lakhdar al-Ibrahimi, accepts that the body has had its ups and downs; it has not been anything like wholly successful. But he believes it has suffered from an in-built contradiction: 'It was supposed to strengthen the independence of individual member states, and it was also intended to make possible Arab unity – which is exactly the opposite of keeping existing states independent. And I believe the Arab League has suffered a little bit from this contradiction.' Mr Ibrahimi went on: 'The League has certainly disappointed the hopes of those who thought this was a step towards the creation of unity. But I think the fact that it has existed has allowed the Arabs to have "their house" (as we say in Arabic); it is the Arab tent. It is the place where Arab governments at all levels meet, discuss their problems and try to organise their co-operation. All in all, it is a very useful organisation, but it cannot be better than the sum total of what the Arab countries are at any one time in their history.'

This inability to act in unison, according to Mr Ibrahimi, is the result of Arab countries being too close to each other. Iceland and the Ivory Coast, for example, have nothing in common and therefore nothing to quarrel about. 'We are much too close to each other to be indifferent towards each other,' he explains, 'The bigger the area of common interest, the bigger the problems and the reasons to differ and quarrel.'

Differences and quarrels. It's very easy to get the impression that there is nothing else to talk about in the Arab world. Certainly most reporting on the region tends to focus on the wars and the countless acts of violence. Up to a point, the Arabs have themselves to blame. Many governments are very reluctant to allow foreign reporters into their countries; even more become very touchy when anything other than what they see as 'positive' news is published. On the other hand, the prejudices which I mentioned at the start of this chapter are as common in Fleet Street as anywhere else. So too, according to most Arabs, is a built-in pro-Israeli bias, with some of the top newspaper bosses being friends of Israel.

Equally, those people in the Western world who try to put forward the Arab cause find themselves fighting a losing battle as they try to explain the motivations behind the stream of Middle East-related acts of terror. There is far more interest in the details of a Palestinian hijacking than there is in the origins and causes of the Palestinian problem.

In the end, one has to look beyond the violence, beyond the squalor of some Arab cities, beyond the unruly mob fighting to get to the check-in desk at a busy airport, beyond all such superficialities which offend and repel many Westerners. For there is one generalisation which one can safely make about the Arabs: as individuals they are hospitable, kind and generous. As one Lebanese lady who had both travelled and lived for long periods outside the Middle East once said: 'I think that, in private, Arabs are very sophisticated, very honest, very generous. I think they have manners which I've found in my travels are lacking in Western countries.'

2 *Islam*

Unity and division

One of my earliest memories is of the Muslim's call to prayer, the chant of the muezzin from the minaret of the mosque. I still find it the sound which evokes most readily the whole atmosphere of the Arab world, whether you hear the voice of the muezzin breaking the dawn silence over Amman, or mingling with the roar of traffic and midday bustle of Cairo, or being punctuated by the sounds of battle in Beirut.

For many foreigners visiting Muslim countries, the call to prayer, in an alien language, with the sound of its alien, ghostly and frightening chant, is a symbol of what they perceive as the mysterious, even threatening nature of Islam. The barriers of ignorance and misunderstanding separating the majority of people in the West and those in the Islamic world are formidable. The West has a host of preconceived ideas about Muslims, the infidels as the Crusaders saw them – ideas which have been fostered by Western literature and culture. Many notions are widespread; that all Muslim women must wear the veil, that Muslim men tend to keep a harem of wives, or that Muslims are fanatical terrorists who carry out suicide bombings – and in any event that they are alien and remote from our own experience.

But in fact the gap between the roots of Christianity and the roots of Islam is surprisingly small. 'Jesus is a very important person in Islam; he's mentioned over thirty times in the Koran,' comments Ahmed Zaki Bedawi of the Muslim College in London. To understand why, one has to look at the origins of Islam in the Arabian peninsula (today's Saudi Arabia) in the seventh century AD.

The Arabian peninsula is almost all desert, so it's a popular concept that Islam is a desert religion. In fact one has to focus on one of the trade routes across the desert and one of the thriving towns on that route: Mecca. It was a cross-roads in every sense, having links with Europe, India and China, and with the cultures and religions of the day: Byzantine, Jewish and Zoroastrian. In Mecca, there was (and is today) a huge cube made of stone blocks called the *Ka'aba*, said to have been built by the prophet Abraham. By the seventh century, however, the Ka'aba had become cluttered with idols, the monotheism of the Jewish faith having been lost. The pagan religions that had sprung up, according to Ahmed Zaki Bedawi, made for attitudes which were out of keeping with a society that had such sophisticated links with other civilisations. For example, human sacrifices were carried out, and women were looked upon with total scorn and treated cruelly. Girl babies were sometimes buried alive.

In 570 Muhammad (also spelled Mohammed, Mahomet or, in Turkish, Mehmed) was born in Mecca. He was engaged in merchant activities until in 610, at the age of forty, he received the prophetic call and soon afterwards (and until his death in 632) began preaching a message that had monotheism (*tawheed*) at its heart. (As it says in the Koran: 'Serve no other gods besides Allah, lest you incur disgrace and ruin'.) This remains the most central and most important theme of Islam today. The idols were removed from the Ka'aba (this building ever since has been the main focus of Islam), the pagan rituals were swept away, and women were given a more respectable role in society.

Muslims believe that Muhammad was the messenger of God and that the words of God were revealed to him through the Archangel Gabriel. These were set down word by word in what became the sacred book, the Koran. The Koran is central to Islamic belief. As Ahmed Zaki Bedawi puts it: 'It was delivered word by word to the people, it was written down and memorised, and is still the most authentic document to this day. There are no disputes about its contents.' The Koran, written in rich classical Arabic (most people would say the finest work in classical Arabic), is universal to all Muslims, regardless of their differences in the interpretation of other aspects of the faith. The Koran itself sets out its own purpose: 'This Koran will guide men to that which is most upright. It promises the believers who do good works a rich reward, and threatens those who deny the life to come a grievous scourge.'

The heart of the Prophet's ministry was that he was the latest in a line of prophets, as chronicled in the Jewish Torah or the Old Testament that ran from Adam through Abraham to Moses and Jesus. He was not only the last, but the most perfect, of this series of messengers. The Muslim belief that, through Muhammad, God gave the final revelation to complete the imperfect religions of Judaism and Christianity, is fundamental – and it is also the single biggest cause of discussion between Islam and the other monotheistic religions. And this is where it's interesting to see the similarities between Islam and Christianity. Both faiths acknowledge Abraham and Moses. The Koran is packed with passages that are familiar to anyone with a knowledge of the Old Testament – the story of Adam and the tree of temptation, for example, or of Joseph and his brothers. Islam accepts too that Jesus was born of Mary by immaculate conception. However, Jesus is regarded by Muslims as another messenger or prophet of God, not as God incarnate. Muslims see God as Creator, and believe that God and Man will always be separate. Also Muslims do not believe that Jesus was crucified, rather that he was lifted up to heaven; and they don't accept the notion of original sin, which leads in turn to the belief that there is no need for sacrifice and redemption. Each individual is responsible for his own sins.

It is interesting too, on the subject of comparisons with Christianity and Judaism, that the Koran exhorts Muslims to be tolerant of the followers of these two religions – 'People of the Book', as they are called. And indeed both were left free to worship after the spread of Islam.

So, a new monotheistic religion, richly steeped in the traditions of the other two great religions, came into being. What is incredible to think of now is how fast this new religion spread out of the Arabian desert city of Mecca. Muhammad was involved in a series of battles with those who rejected his teaching and by the time of his death he had united a number of nomadic tribes behind him, won several victories, and united most of Arabia. So the faith was entrenched and ready for carrying further afield into Syria and Iraq. And within decades of the death of the Prophet Muhammad, Islam (the word means submission – to God, of course) was spreading north and west along North Africa and eventually into Spain (Spain was a Muslim country for 700 years), up into the Levant and into Turkey and eastern Europe, and east into Persia. Ahmed Zaki Bedawi believes the spread was so rapid in part because Islam is a 'simple doctrine, it's very easy for people to understand. There are few mysteries. And that allowed Islam to embody a lot of cultures along the way.' Also, once its early years had passed it met very little resistance. The big powers of the day, the Byzantine and Persian empires, were in decline, and it was relatively easy for Islam to conquer both. Today, Islam may have largely lost its hold in Europe (though Bosnia in Yugoslavia has a sizeable Muslim population and many working mosques), but there are reckoned, in all, to be over 500 million Muslims in the world, the majority spread in a great sweep of the earth's surface between Morocco in the west and Indonesia in the east.

For these millions the five pillars or simple, fundamental bases of Islam are:

- repeating the basic utterance of the Faith: there is no god but God and Muhammad is the messenger of God;
- daily prayer;
- payment of obligatory alms ('zakah') for the poor;
- observation of the religious festival of Ramadan;
- pilgrimage ('mass') to Mecca at least once in one's life for those who can afford it.

In addition the Koran is an important binding force. One can hear it recited, in Arabic, wherever Islam is practised. A great unifying factor too is prayer. Muslims are required to pray five times a day and, in what I find a very moving sense of community, they are required to face Mecca – or to be more specific, the Ka'aba at Mecca. Some hotels in the Arab world mark with an arrow the direction of Mecca. In one in Oman, a prayer mat is provided with a compass fixed to one corner. I saw a building worker in Cairo, for example, stop work and, amid the rubble, spread a cloth on the ground before facing Mecca and going through the motions of prayer, bending forward, kneeling and touching the ground with his forehead, and quietly mouthing the prayers. He must have gained great strength from the thought that exactly the same private act of worship was being carried out all through the Arab world and much further afield too. It is as well to be aware of this sense of religious community in the Arab world which can so often override political differences.

The idea of one God, the recognition of the Prophet, the acceptance of the Koran and the acts of worship – such signs of unity are crowned by the pilgrimage to Mecca. It is the duty of every Muslim to perform the pilgrimage to Mecca once in his lifetime, provided that he has the means to be able to do so.

These days, hundreds of thousands of people reach Saudi Arabia by air to perform the pilgrimage. Airlines run charter flights from all over the world which arrive at a special terminal at Jeddah airport. From Jeddah, fleets of buses take the pilgrims along dual carriageways lined with advertising boards, eastwards towards Mecca. As the buses approach the city, overhead signs indicate that non-Muslims must veer off to the right; only Muslims are allowed to enter, and all traffic passes through a control point where checks are made on the religion of the passengers.

A religious barrier there may be. But there's no bar on nationalities. David Cowan is a quietly spoken Scot. For many years he taught at the School of Oriental and African Studies at London University and wrote one of the leading books on Arabic grammar. He's now retired. But long before he became a leading Arabic scholar he adopted the Islamic faith. In fact, he was sixteen at the time, and his first contact with Islam was through the reading he did in the library in his home city of Dundee. He first performed the pilgrimage in 1949. Since then he's been known to his friends, in the same way that all pilgrims are, as Hajji – literally, the man who has performed the *Hajj*, or pilgrimage. From Hajji Daoud (the Arabic equivalent of David) and from other Muslims it's possible to create a picture of the Hajj.

Women are free to wear the clothes they wish, but men traditionally wear a simple one-piece white garment, devoid of frills. The simplicity of the garments and the fact that they are worn by all male pilgrims help to break down national or class barriers, and contribute to the sense of Muslim unity. Many pilgrims are not sure what exactly to do in Mecca, so there are guides to teach them how to perform the pilgrimage. The first duty after praying in the sacred mosque is to walk seven times round the Ka'aba saying prayers in praise and glorification of God. In the north-east of the Ka'aba you see a black stone encircled in silver which is said to have been placed there by Abraham. Each time you pass the black stone you are supposed to kiss it, not to venerate it, but to make physical contact with a symbol of the roots of Islam. Because of the enormous crowds, some pilgrims don't get a chance to kiss the stone and have to be content with making a gesture to it. Then the pilgrims walk seven times along a marble pavement between two nearby hills called Safa and Marwa, after which they are said to have performed the lesser pilgrimage. On the eighth day of the month of pilgrimage (the last month in the Muslim calendar) the pilgrims go to a high plain just outside Mecca called Arafat. On the following day they stand praying or reading the Koran from midday until sunset. Finally the crowd, sometimes some two million strong, will leave, shepherded away by the Saudi police. All who perform the pilgrimage say they are moved by the experience, especially the experience of meeting and mixing with so many different nationalities and races bound by the one religion. There is also a sense of continuity of history. Here the worshippers find themselves at a spot made sacred by Abraham, centuries before the birth of Islam, and yet inherited by Islam through the experience of the Prophet Muhammad.

There is no hierarchy in Islam in the way that Christianity has its priesthood. Matters are left far more to the individual, who is guided by scholars. Among scholars there is a hierarchy, based on reputation and experience. Titles like 'Ayatollah' which one hears in Iran are accorded on the basis of achievement in the scholarly world rather than power bestowed directly by God. Indeed it is the right of any Muslim to challenge the views of the scholars. They are not regarded as absolute authorities. Nor are they invested with the power, for example, to grant absolution of sins.

Thus it is as wrong to make generalisations about the practices of Islam as it is about Arabs and the Arab world. The roots of Islam are common to all Muslims; but the interpretations differ from area to area, from country to country, from individual to individual. Just as some Christians go to church every Sunday, so some Muslims go to communal prayers at the mosque at midday on Fridays. (Mosques are not consecrated buildings as churches are, but are more like combined places of prayer and social centres, where many kinds of issues outside religion are discussed.) In some parts of the Arab world Muslims will adhere much more strictly to the requirement to fast during the Muslim month of Ramadan than in others. The duty is that one should take no food or water from first light until sunset (though exceptions are made for certain people – e.g. pregnant women). At sunset, the Koran directs: 'Eat and drink until you can tell a white thread from a black one in the light of the coming dawn.' Foreigners in Muslim countries are not required to fast, but are expected to show respect by refraining from eating or smoking in public during the hours of fasting. Ramadan falls about ten days earlier every year, and its observance is particularly demanding when the festival falls in the long and extremely hot days of summer. Muslims also differ in the extent to which they observe the dictum that it is the duty of all Muslims to give alms (one-fortieth of their capital) to the poor and needy.

In everyday life too there are major variations in practice. The question of the rights of women is a good example. It is true, as everyone in the West must know, that a Muslim man is entitled to take four wives. But the strict condition is that he must be able to maintain them on an equal basis, a condition that these days very, very few people are able to meet. So to find a man in the Arab world with even two wives is indeed rare. In general, as we have seen, Islam did much to improve the lot of women in society, and many Muslim women these days dismiss the common view in the West that they are second-class citizens, despite the existence of a women's movement in some countries which is pressing for more radical reforms. Mrs Afaf Eissa is a Sudanese living in London. She is a strict Muslim with three children. She believes that women are equal partners within the marriage, but women accept that the role of mother and spiritual guide to the children comes first. And as for one of the other common stereotype views of Muslim women, that they are forced to wear veils and keep out of sight, Mrs Eissa – wearing a head-scarf and Western dress has this to say: 'I think it's more the tradition of a particular country than a matter of religion. In general, Islam expects a woman to look respectable in her clothes, covering the head and body.' The same goes for such adornments as make-up: 'It's fine to look good and comfortable, but without going out with the intention of attracting other men's attention.'

This mixture of religion with social and cultural tradition is part of what makes the Arab world so rich and varied, and it explains why generalities are usually inaccurate. The custom that keeps women veiled and largely segregated from men in Saudi Arabia does not apply in Tunis, for example, where male and female students wear Western-type clothes and mix freely. Both societies are founded on Islam.

These variations appear not just in matters of practice, but in more basic interpretations as well. Up to now I have avoided mention of the major split within Islam which occurred shortly after its birth in the seventh century. It's the split that has separated the Shiia (predominant in Iran, the majority Muslim community in Iraq, the biggest single religious group in Lebanon, and found in smaller numbers in other Arab states) from the Sunnis (by far the majority throughout the Arab world). Roughly speaking, more than ninety per cent of Muslims are Sunnis, fewer than ten per cent Shiia. Muslim scholars like Ahmed Zaki Bedawi like to play down the differences between the two: 'It's a very minor issue. The distance which divides them is very small. They don't differ on the key concepts such as the Koran, Muhammad, God, the acts of worship – not on any fundamental theological issue at all. The only difference of any fundamental value is how the Muslims run their estate.'

During his lifetime, Muhammad created not just a religion but a state as well. He united most of Arabia as its spiritual and political head. When he died his function of prophet ended, but his position as head of state had to be continued. A dispute about how his successor (in Arabic *Khalifa* or *Caliph*) should be chosen led to the first major split in the new religion. There were essentially two views: one argued that because the Prophet had been chosen by God and not elected by the community, his successor too should be chosen by God and the community had no authority. This group decided that God had made the choice of Ali, the cousin and son-in-law of the Prophet, and that the succession should carry on through his line. This was the view adopted by the Shiia (from the Arabic *Shiiat Ali*, or followers of Ali).

A different view was adopted by the Sunnis (*Sunna* in Arabic meaning custom or path). They believed God meant that the community of Muslims should decide the succession. The Sunnis have tended to be regarded as the 'orthodox' Muslims, while the Shiia have at times been persecuted for their faith. In addition, a number of smaller sects have broken off from the Shiia over the centuries, for example, the Alawis (the ruling minority group in Syria) and the Ismailis (the spiritual head of one group of them being the Agha Khan). To look in detail at any more than the main groups within Islam would be a long and complicated study.

Differences in outlook, differences in interpretation: at times these have sparked off great controversy, at times great bloodshed. The basic Islamic law (in Arabic *Shari'a*) is highly complicated. The Koran itself does specify certain punishments for certain crimes, and lays down some legal procedures covering, in general, matters like theft, illicit sex ('The adulterer and the adulteress shall each be given a hundred lashes') and other crimes which occurred in seventh-century Arabia. It also lays down directions for such subjects as inheritance, and such personal matters as diet, breast-feeding and menstruation. But the legal content of the Koran is limited. And a much broader body of law was soon needed to match the size and complexities of the new Arab empire. So it was left to the scholars in the two centuries following Muhammad's death to formulate the Shari'a as commanded (explicitly or implicitly) by God – and to build up a vast body of legislation to cover matters not referred to in the Koran, on the basis of what they thought the Koran meant, and on the basis of the way the Prophet behaved and what he said, or was meant to have said. Such a system is, of course, wide open for huge differences in interpretation and disagreement. There is a whole science, for example, in the study of the reliability of the sayings of the Prophet, some categorised as very reliable, others less reliable, others a bit doubtful, and so on. Therefore it was possible on certain subjects to find a saying (in Arabic *Hadeeth*) which suited your particular point of view, and for that assessment to be challenged by another scholar on the grounds that the Hadeeth was unreliable. For instance, it's the result of such differences of interpretation that the drinking of alcohol is allowed in countries like Tunisia and Morocco, and not in Kuwait or Saudi Arabia.

The other problem has come with the arrival of the modern age. A body of law which evolved out of mediaeval Arabia began to be inappropriate for countries absorbing the fruits of the industrial revolution and being subjected suddenly to the liberal thinking of the West. Indeed, the past century, since the Arab world was opened up to the West, has seen Middle East countries trying to cope with the dilemma: how far should one try to adapt Shari'a law to suit modern needs, and how much should one replace it with secular law?

There have been major differences of opinion over this. Take the example so often quoted in the West – that a thief should have his hand cut off, as required under Shari'a law. Some scholars earlier this century argued that such punishments need not be followed in a narrow and literal way; rather they were examples that might have been appropriate at a time before prisons or other punishments were common. Other scholars disagreed, and in Saudi Arabia the traditional punishments are still applied, albeit under modern medical supervision. Supporters of the traditional way of life argue that there is sufficient material on which to cope with the practices of modern life. Take birth control, for example. Charles Gai Eaton, an author and convert to Islam, quotes a Hadeeth of the Prophet (considered reliable) that the Prophet's companions told him they practised coitus interruptus because, while big families were and are encouraged, they felt they had enough children. The Prophet responded without comment and his silence was taken to mean that under certain circumstances, birth control was deemed to be acceptable even if not particularly approved of. The same attitude applies to divorce.

The degree to which Arab countries have retained or rejected Islamic law varies considerably. In summary form, Malise Ruthven, who has made a study of the whole subject, puts it like this: 'On the whole those countries like Egypt with long histories of foreign influences have tended to adopt modified forms of European codes of law, leaving Islamic law to matters of personal status, and so on. Countries in the Arabian peninsula, on the other hand, which were least influenced from outside, have kept Islamic law more or less intact.'

There is today a strong movement among modern Islamic scholars and thinkers to try to build a universal Islamic order. The Islamic Council is spearheading this movement, having produced a declaration of human rights for Muslims and a model Islamic constitution. One of its leaders, Selim Azzam, spelt out a belief that is common among many scholars and religious leaders: 'No single Arab country is applying Islam correctly, even if they say they are. In reality, their deeds and actions are completely contrary to Islamic principles.' Given the fact that we tend to think of the Arab world as being the heart of the Islamic world, this might seem an astonishing statement. The Islamic Council justifies the need for action of this kind by pointing out that as a body it is not welcome in a single Arab state.

There is certainly a vociferous body of opinion calling for a return to old traditional, fundamental Islamic ideals, and the Muslim fundamentalist movement has come very much to the fore in recent years. From time to time, Arab regimes have been forced to make cosmetic changes to accommodate their demands. In Egypt, for example, President Sadat announced radical amendments to the divorce laws, giving women the same rights as men. Malise Ruthven says that it was partly under pressure from Muslim fundamentalists that the Supreme Court in Egypt under his successor, President Mubarak, revoked Sadat's amendments.

The trend towards Islamic fundamentalism (both Sunni and Shiia) was given a big boost by the Islamic (Shiia) revolution in Iran which toppled the Shah. It was certainly the inspiration for the Shiia community in southern Lebanon in the mid-1980s. It gave men and women the courage to carry out daring suicide attacks. (To die in the cause of a 'holy war' – a *jihad* – guarantees a place in paradise.) But Islam in that case was first and foremost a rallying point to deal with a perceived injustice, i.e. the Israeli occupation of their land. There is no doubt that in the minds of many people in the West, the association of Islam with terror springs from a mis-understanding of the motives of a particular act of violence. Islam may be a vehicle, even a catalyst. But it is rarely the cause.

Similarly, the renewed interest in Islam in Egypt and elsewhere reflects a natural tendency to turn to the familiar for comfort at times of adversity, whether the causes be poverty, hunger, homelessness or war – fuelled perhaps by disillusionment at the promises (offered, but never fulfilled) of greater benefits which will result from closer ties with the West, or fuelled by disgust at the corruption and hypocrisy of certain Arab regimes which claim to rule in the name of Islam. For whatever the outward appearances, at heart the over-whelming majority of Arabs are Muslims, and have the instincts of a Muslim – no matter how grand or lowly that Muslim may be. Professor Fouad Ajami, in his book *The Arab Predicament*, explains how the defeat of the Arabs in the 1967 war with Israel marked the defeat of the era of secular Arab nationalism which had been espoused above all by President Nasser of Egypt: 'The shock of the military defeat created a deep need for solace and consolation, and Islam provided the needed comfort. The phenomenon was strongest in Egypt, but the same thing happened throughout the Arab world. Sensing the new mood, the previously more or less secular pan-Arabists began to display greater piety.'

Disillusionment with society, politics and the quality of life are making many more people in the Arab world take an interest in religion than in past years. This is particularly noticeable among the young. In parts of Egypt matters have gone even further, with something akin to an alternative social system being set up, with Islamic schools, hospitals and other institutions offering services to the people. They are popular not so much because of their Islamic character, but because they are providing services which compare very favourably with those offered (or in some cases not offered) by the state. In other words, Islam is seen to be caring when the state, for financial or bureaucratic reasons, is not.

I believe that the alarm felt in the West by this revival of interest in Islam is not justified. Muslim hordes are not about to descend on Europe. Islam in the Arab world, like Christianity in Europe or the United States, is an important strand in the fabric of society. At certain times that strand is more in evidence than at others.

(Quotations from the Koran are taken from the translation by N. J. Dawood published by Penguin (1983).)

3 Egypt

The heart-beat of the Arab world

Egypt provides the heart-beat and the humour of the Arab world. The land of pharaohs and pyramids, of the treasures of Tutankhamun, of the faded glory of Alexandria which Lawrence Durrell called 'that strange and evocative city'. It is a land dominated by Cairo, a sprawling shambles of a city squatting on the banks of the Nile, a city of maddening and almost permanent traffic jams, unspeakable squalor and flashes of sublime beauty wrapped in smog and the smells of poverty. It is a land of simple but hard peasant life, of women washing their clothes in the murky river water, glancing at the luxury cruise boat passing by; the land of the Coptic church; the land of the pencil-thin canal which cuts through the desert, linking Port Said and Suez, the Mediterranean and the Red Sea, the north and the south, the channel between two worlds; the land of cinema, theatre and song; the land of choking bureaucracy and overwhelmingly warm friendship and hospitality; the land of President Nasser and Sadat, of cafés and political talk; a land which is the heart of the Arab world and much more. You must love Egypt or hate it. It's too big and overpowering for indifference.

Egypt, quite simply, is the giant of the Arab world in every sense, regardless of the fact that in political terms it went through a period of partial isolation because of the signing by President Anwar Sadat in 1979 of the peace treaties with Israel, the treaties labelled the 'Camp David' accords after the long hours of discussion that took place at President Carter's summer retreat in the days leading up to the signing ceremony. Egypt is big in every way, and its position, as near to the hub of the Arab world as it is possible to get, has caused it to have a profound influence on the way of life in the surrounding countries which was bound to outweigh short-term political differences.

The population of Egypt stands at around fifty million, making it by far the most populous Arab state. Its capital is the largest city by far in the Arab world – and perhaps the second or third largest in the world. Furthermore it is a country which has to face the continuing nightmare of having to find food, jobs and homes for a

continually expanding population. Every nine or ten months another million are added to the total. And this, as we shall see, lies at the root of Egypt's considerable economic difficulties.

Egypt is made up mostly of desert; for centuries the population has lived and worked in towns and villages along the thin fertile strip which is the Nile, and in the Nile delta region to the north where the river opens into the sea like a giant fan. This clinging to the life-giving artery can be seen easily from the air: a thin green line stencilled onto an area of emptiness – the Eastern and Western Deserts. By far the biggest population centre is the capital, Cairo. It is estimated that between ten and fifteen million people are squeezed into this still largely antiquated city which was built for a population a fraction of the size. Cairo is a jumble of architectural styles, ranging from the poorest shanty dwellings, through the ornate colonial architecture from the Victorian period, through the stark eastern European-modelled 'modern' buildings of the 1950s to the skyscraper hotels and offices of the 1980s.

The Cairenes and those who troop into the city in search of work find accommodation according to the money in their pockets. For the rich in their fashionable European clothes and smart cars there is a choice of splendid villas overlooking the Nile or tucked away in smart suburbs like Heliopolis or Maadi. At night they can be tempted by five-star hotel restaurants or a choice of night-clubs. The rich account for only a small percentage of the population, but within their grasp they hold a disproportionate and growing amount of the nation's wealth.

For the majority of the population, however, life is a considerable struggle, a struggle made even tougher with the passing years by inflation and rising prices. Families have no choice but to cram into dilapidated houses or bleak high-rise blocks of flats. Each day they must face the morass of Cairo traffic jams in their old and dented cars, or in the old and dented buses and trams constantly packed to overflowing as they crawl through the dusty heat, which provide the backbone of the public transport system. For the remainder it's a question of finding a place to sleep – any kind of place. So it is that many thousands (some say over a million) of Egyptians spend their nights in shanty towns or – in one well-publicised case – among the grave-stones in one of the city's cemetries, the so-called 'City of the Dead'. And at first light, as the sun begins its battle to break through the mist and smog, you can see these ghostly figures in their ragged *galabiya* crowding round the little stalls which sell *foul* – the beans which make up the staple diet of the Egyptians. In the countryside too, the poverty is appalling to see. The impression of most people coming to Egypt for the first time, seeing the chaos of Cairo and the backward conditions in the villages outside, is one of astonishment that the country manages to get by from day to day. Nobody seems to know how it happens. Unlike any other Arab country, Egypt seems ungovernable, unworkable, with its soaring population, its chronic shortage of jobs and housing, and its mounting foreign debt.

Egypt's survival thus far has been helped greatly by the ability of other Arab countries to absorb a large share of the Egyptian workforce. It's reckoned that around three million Egyptians work abroad, with about half this figure finding jobs in Iraq and the Gulf states. Consequently, Egypt too has been affected by the problem which is besetting all the states in the region these days one way or another: the sudden and sharp drop in the price of oil. Not only has the price of Egypt's own oil (produced largely in the Sinai desert) fallen, but many of the foreign workers have been put out of work in the Gulf states. This has meant a drop in remittances from abroad (a key source of foreign earnings) and the return of the workers from other countries, thus increasing the number of people unemployed at home.

But somehow, despite the problems, Egypt ticks along. Perhaps it's the momentum of so many centuries of history that keeps it going. Every tourist who visits Egypt has seen the Pyramids of Giza just outside Cairo and the other spectacular relics of ancient history such as the Valley of the Kings in the ancient city of Thebes and the Temples of Karnak and Abu Simbel. It is a history that goes back to the Pharaonic, Greek and Roman periods, then leads up to the arrival of Islam. The discovery earlier this century of the tomb of Tutankhamun in the Valley of the Kings provided a spectacular icing to the rich cake of archaeological finds that are displayed in the National Museum in Cairo – a museum which is a monument to the decades of civilisations, ancient and modern, that have contributed to the soul of Egypt. Alexander the Great conquered Egypt in 332 BC and built the port city on the Mediterranean shore which bears his name. Alexander was followed by the Ptolemaic dynasty, which is celebrated in popular historic terms by the reign of Cleopatra. Then came the Romans, in an era which saw the establishment of the Coptic church in Egypt – a church which survived the arrival of Islam in the seventh century and still survives today, despite several periods of tension between it and the Muslim-dominated state apparatus.

In the thirteenth century the Mameluks (meaning 'the owned ones', i.e. slaves), who were mainly of Turkish origin, came to power, but in the sixteenth century Egypt, like so many areas of the Arab world, became part of the Ottoman empire. The major change of direction came in 1798 when Napoleon and his army occupied Egypt with the aim of disrupting the British trade link with India. He was eventually forced to retreat, but not before doors to the modern world had been opened in Egypt. After the stagnation of the Ottoman period, young Egyptians were suddenly presented with French culture and political thought. The man credited with the distinction of being the 'architect of modern Egypt' was an officer of Albanian extraction named Muhammed Ali. He was Pasha from 1805 to 1849, and in that time encouraged the development of education and other European ideas which formed the basis of a system which would rear the nationalist thinkers of the next century.

One of the most significant developments of the nineteenth century was the digging of the Suez Canal. In 1856, a Frenchman called Ferdinand de Lesseps was given the go-ahead to build the canal. Work began in 1859 and finished ten years later – an event which was marked by huge celebrations in Cairo. The festivities were to have included a performance of *Aïda* which had been commissioned for the occasion, but the opera was not finished in time. (The Cairo opera house where it was eventually performed was burnt to the ground in the 1970s.) Despite the French involvement in the construction of the canal, Britain gained control of it, having bought up Egypt's share in its development to help the country out of a financial crisis and an agreement was signed in 1882 stating that the canal was to remain under British control for 99 years.

This action marked the beginning of the era of British domination of Egyptian affairs. It also marked the beginning of a struggle between the government in Westminster and the nationalist leaders both while they were seeking independence and later when they came to power, a struggle which characterised Egyptian politics of the first half of the twentieth century. The first shots in the struggle were fired in 1881 when a group of Egyptian army officers, inspired by the first stirrings of nationalist ambitions, led by Arabi Pasha, forced the leader of the day, Tawfik, to put nationalist figures into top jobs, despite warnings from Britain that he should not do so. When Tawfik gave in to the strong anti-British feelings which were growing in Egypt, the British sent an expeditionary forced which landed at Ismailia and later defeated the Egyptian army. The earlier appointments were then rescinded.

Britain continued to retain control in Egypt and, at the start of the First World War in 1914, the country formally became a British protectorate under the control of a High Commissioner. But all the time, nationalist feelings were growing, and the gap between the British authorities and the Egyptian leaders whom Britain backed was widening. In 1922 Egypt was declared an independent monarchy, with King Fuad upon the newly created throne, but it was independent in name only, with British troops remaining on Egyptian soil and security of the Suez Canal still under the wing of Whitehall. With each year that passed, the popularity of the monarchy declined, while the nationalists won increasing support. The King and his British advisers juggled with 'tame' nationalist leaders to try to meet popular demands, but they were only putting off what was inevitable.

Before independence was finally achieved, however, Egypt found itself caught up in the Second World War. This period has given Egypt a secure place in British history books – the battle of El-Alamein being perhaps the best chronicled of all the events of those days. It was a period which also saw direct and raw contact between young British soldiers and ordinary Egyptians and was instrumental in forming many of the impressions of 'the Arabs' which are still firmly fixed in British minds. Many of the troops displayed scarcely disguised racist attitudes to 'the bloody Gyppos', yet some kind of rapport seems to have developed since, if nothing else, words like 'bint' and 'shufti' have entered English slang. A couple of years ago, while visiting that dusty but delightful relic of colonial days, Port Said, at a café close to a building on which – despite the grime – I could read the carved inscription 'The British Foreign Bible Society', I was approached by a shoe-shine man. He was old and crippled, and his leathery arms were covered in tattoos. 'Shoes cleaned, sir?', he said 'I'll give 'em one 'ell of a shine.' It was straight out of the British barrack-room and the old man had indeed worked for the British troops. Egypt is full of such reminders of every chapter of its history.

After the war, King Farouk became fatter and more corrupt, and Britain began to feel more and more uncomfortable in the atmosphere of growing hostility. The end came on 23 July 1952 when a group of young officers in Cairo seized power in a bloodless coup. King Farouk simply sailed away into exile, his departure mourned by no more than a handful of Egyptians. The 'Free Officers' who had planned and successfully carried out the coup were led by Colonel Abdel Nasser, yet Egypt's first president was General Muhammed Neguib. In the early months, Nasser stayed on the sidelines, waiting to see which way things were going, but a struggle developed between him and Neguib, the former advocating a future for Egypt based on socialism and Arab nationalism, the latter being more conservative and religious in temperament. In November 1954 Neguib was accused of having associations with the extremist Sunni Muslim group known as the Muslim Brotherhood. He was arrested, and Nasser became President.

Egypt settled down to a decade which was marked by a blossoming of self-confidence, boosted by the brilliant rhetoric of President Nasser which was broadcast by the Voice of the Arabs radio station in Cairo to every country in the Arab world. President Nasser, nurturing dreams of Arab unity with which to confront Western imperialism, took pleasure in taunting Europe (in particular Britain) and the United States. He became one of the most influential and most talked-about leaders in the world, quickly establishing Egypt's position as the fountain of ideas for pan-Arab secularism, opening up links with Eastern bloc and African states, and becoming a leading figure in the non-aligned movement.

Political exuberance, however, was not enough to overcome Egypt's traditional economic problems. President Nasser believed that one solution to these would be to increase the amount of land on which food could be grown by building a high dam at Aswan. The United States, with some help from Britain, agreed to pay for the building of the dam, but with a certain amount of unease since both were angered by the anti-Western rhetoric coming out of Cairo. So when Nasser denounced the Baghdad Pact agreement in 1956 (a move which caused, among other things, the removal of Glubb Pasha from Jordan and infuriated the British Prime Minister, Sir Anthony Eden), the Americans backed out of their agreement to finance the project. This prompted President Nasser to take one of the most important and controversial decisions in the history of Egypt. He announced that Egypt was nationalising the Suez Canal and would finance the dam itself with the money coming from revenues from the canal. Britain was outraged, but no-one in that country more so than Sir Anthony Eden, who seemed to believe that Nasser had taken the decision specifically to rile him.

From then on Eden decided that, at whatever cost, Nasser must be stopped and removed from power. It became a personal obsession which lost him friends and respect both inside his own government and civil service and among his foreign allies. When the United Nations and international efforts of all kinds failed to break the will and determination of President Nasser, Sir Anthony began thinking of military action. He did not receive the key support of the United States for this, although documentation has subsequently shown that he chose to think that he had it.

In any event, in the following days Britain and France became involved in one of the most shameful acts of international deception in their two histories, the full details of which weren't known for many years. They agreed that the Israelis should launch an attack against Egypt, the pretext being to retaliate for cross-border commando raids. Britain and France, as guarantor powers, called on both countries to withdraw to positions on either side of the canal. Israel agreed, but Egypt refused. And in the face of overwhelming international hostility, in October 1956 Britain and France began launching air attacks on Egypt. A few months before, Britain had pulled its last troops out of Egypt; but by November some of them were back, coming ashore at Port Said.

At this point, following strong American and European pressure, a ceasefire was agreed on, and within days the British forces had withdrawn. It was an unhappy adventure for Britain. The former colonial power had been publicly humiliated; Sir Anthony Eden in particular felt bitter and angry. The ripples from that particular foreign policy fiasco did not die down for years, either in Britain or in the Arab world.

The affair left President Nasser the hero of the Arabs and their undisputed leader, and in this atmosphere he tried to build on his notions of pan-Arabism while at the same time developing closer links with the Eastern bloc countries. The Soviet Union built the Aswan high dam, provided huge quantities of arms and posted thousands of military advisers to Egypt. The euphoria did not, however, produce the desired result. Egypt's economy and bureacracy became leaden as a result of widespread nationalisation. The President was forced to deal firmly with opposition both from communists and religious extremists; and his attempts at political union with Syria (The United Arab Republic 1958–1963) failed, as did plans for a unified political command with Iraq.

But still these set-backs were nothing compared with the disaster of the June 1967 Arab–Israeli war (the Six Day War). This was pre-cipitated by President Nasser's announcement that Israeli shipping would not be allowed to proceed up the Gulf of Aqaba to Eilat. Despite the backing which Egypt received from Jordan and Syria, who co-ordinated their attacks with Cairo, the war was an unmitigated disaster for Egypt and for the Arabs as a whole. The Egyptian air force was more or less wiped out before it could take off, and the Sinai peninsula fell to Israel.

The defeat destroyed President Nasser. He wanted to resign, but was prevented from doing so by a huge and emotional display of public support. However, he never recovered from the humiliation of that defeat. The President, one suspects, knew that it spelt the end of an era. The dream of the Arabs rising up to defeat the Zionist enemy were shattered once and for all. He died in 1970, a sick man with a broken spirit. Millions of people took to the streets of Cairo to mourn their fallen hero.

His successor was another of the officers who had taken part in the 1952 coup which toppled the monarch – Anwar Sadat. He was as different from Nasser as it was possible to be. And he changed the course of his country. Sadat was a man who loved publicity and enjoyed making the kind of bold (his enemies said 'rash') decisions which attracted that publicity. One such move was the decision in 1972 to expel the Russian military advisers. Thenceforth Egypt was to look to the West for economic and military assistance. President Sadat introduced an 'open door' policy designed to attract Western investment – it worked. Foreign companies built hotels and banks in Egypt; but the policy did very little to help those millions at the bottom end of the economic scale. The rich got richer and the poor got poorer.

At that time the 1967 defeat still hung heavily over Egypt. The country was in an unsettling position of 'no war, no peace'. President Sadat kept promising revenge, but it never seemed to come – until 6 October 1973, when the President pulled off one of his most daring and successful surprises. Egyptian troops did what the Israelis had believed to be impossible. They crossed the Suez Canal and caught the Israeli forces off guard. For a day or two Israel seemed to be in very real trouble. Only urgent assistance from the United States in the form of badly needed equipment and ammunition saved Israel from what could have been a defeat. In the end the 1973 war was not a military victory for Egypt, but it was a psychological victory. And it was a personal triumph for President Sadat.

For a time it looked as though the President was in an unassailable position. But Egypt's old problems kept reappearing. Most notably the hungry were getting hungrier. Bread riots and student unrest in the universities provided challenges to the presidency. True to form, though, with his back against the wall, President Sadat in November 1977 pulled off the most dramatic and unexpected coup of his life by flying to Jerusalem to address the Knesset – the first Arab leader ever to do so. The Israelis and the Americans, among others, were overjoyed at seeing the mould broken. The Arabs were shocked and outraged. The President, they believed, had sold the Arab soul to the enemy. President Sadat, however, was not put off by the criticisms. He believed that his dramatic gesture was the opening of a new era of peace in the Middle East and that, in the end, history would prove he had been right. Over the next two years, with the encouragement of President Carter, Anwar Sadat and Prime Minister Menachim Begin of Israel thrashed out the Camp David agreements. Under these, the two countries agreed never to go to war again; the Sinai was to be returned to Egyptian control; and self-determination was to be granted eventually to Palestinians living under occupation in the

West Bank and Gaza strip. For the first time, Israel and an Arab country established diplomatic relations.

The Arab world was enraged. As I have mentioned in Chapter One, they united to break off official links with Cairo and the Arab League moved its headquarters from Cairo to Tunis. President Sadat found himself receiving the highest accolades that the international community could bestow upon him. But, to a considerable extent within his own country, and most certainly within the Arab world as a whole, he was in a political wilderness. At home the President promised that the agreement would bring extra American aid and therefore greater prosperity for everyone. This was not to be the case. The extra aid arrived, but not the prosperity. And more and more, those Egyptians who criticised the Camp David accord were suppressed. President Sadat became increasingly remote from his people and increasingly authoritarian. Muslim extremists and liberal intellectuals were detained by the score.

It was, in fact, a Muslim fundamentalist who led the attack during a military parade in Cairo on 6 October 1981 which killed the President. The world was shocked. They had become used to seeing the urbane Egyptian leader puffing on his pipe and smiling before the television cameras. He was everything the West wanted an Egyptian president to be; but he had become deaf to the complaints of a large section of the Egyptian people.

I arrived in Cairo at dawn on the morning after the assassination wondering what I would find. In the event there was an eerie calm over the city. No mourning, no celebration. Just a hint of anxiety. Vice-president Hosni Mubarak, who had escaped injury though sitting only a few chairs away on the same podium as Sadat, had assumed power. On the surface, life seemed to be continuing normally. But the funeral was anything but normal by Egyptian standards. During the funeral of the previous President, Nasser, people had been crushed to death in the swarming, hysterical crowds. On this day, during a lengthy drive throughout the city I saw not a single person mourning. Not a single ordinary Egyptian attended the burial, which took place yards away from where the President had been killed. President Carter was there; so too were Menachem Begin and dozens of other world leaders and dignitaries. But no ordinary Egyptians.

President Mubarak, still in control six years later, has provided yet another contrast. He has been perhaps what Egypt needed after the flamboyant style of Sadat. President Mubarak is an air force pilot by profession (Commander of the Air Force and hero of the 1973 war) and is calm and softly spoken where Sadat was excitable and prone to emotional outbursts of joy or anger. The army, the key institution in the country, appears to be loyal to the President, apparently respecting his straightforward and practical style of leadership. President Mubarak has gone some way to correct some of the excesses of the Sadat era. Most detainees have been freed, for example, and members of President Sadat's family and entourage have been prosecuted for corruption. However, the biggest legacy, the peace treaty with Israel, remains in existence, even if Egypt in recent times has not been looking at it with as much enthusiasm as Israel and the United States would like. And in September 1986 President Mubarak ended the period of so-called 'cold peace' by meeting the then Israeli Prime Minister, Mr Shimon Peres, for the first time. Simultaneously Mubarak has been trying to mend fences with the rest of the Arab world; it was an important psychological boost to Egypt when Jordan decided in 1986 to re-establish full diplomatic ties with Egypt, even though there was disappointment that other states did not follow suit.

Once again one of the major difficulties which President Mubarak faces, as his predecessors did, is how to deal with the ailing economy. Egypt faces a very serious external debt problem. World bodies have urged the country to cut subsidies on bread, basic foods, electricity and fuel as a condition for receiving more aid. But history has shown on a number of occasions that to try to remove subsidies provokes public anger which can easily be exploited by disaffected public groups within society. In 1977 President Sadat was forced to cancel an order cutting bread subsidies because of the bloody riots it provoked. President Mubarak has been successful in shaving some subsidies here and there. But few observers think that any Egyptian leader would have the courage to slash them all.

In the meantime the traditional sources of foreign earnings have all been coming under strain. Tourism has suffered because of the rise of terrorism in the Mediterranean and Middle East areas. The dues on ships sailing through the Suez Canal are down because of the recession in the Gulf, and remittances from foreign workers there and elsewhere have fallen. On top of this, Egypt's own oil production is down. The beginning of 1986 saw more riots, this time by young conscripts of the central security police. It was not, as some people at the time predicted, followed by mass lawlessness. But it was a terrifying sign of what lurks below the surface.

In politics too there are worries. President Mubarak has allowed more political opposition than was permitted by his predecessor, but the worsening economy combined with continuing hostility to the Camp David agreements have meant a good many Egyptians continue to feel disaffected. Unless improvements come soon that disaffection could spill over into the streets. Worrying too for the Egyptian leadership is the growing strength of fundamentalist Muslims. In the eyes of many poor Egyptians neither the socialism of President Nasser's days, nor the Western-oriented capitalist policies of Presidents Sadat and Mubarak have done anything to improve their lot. So religion is all they have to cling to.

Looked at in these terms Egyptians don't seem to have much too smile at. And yet the Egyptians quite rightly enjoy the reputation of being the best-humoured and most sociable of all the Arabs. Their songs, their plays, their television soap-operas and their jokes (often at their own expense) are loved in every place where Arabic is spoken. In culture and entertainment, as in every other way, Egypt is too big to be ignored.

4 Lebanon

The devastated country

We were just getting off the Beirut airport bus to board the plane when the first shell crashed onto the tarmac. Along with the other passengers we scrambled up the steps. On board, the cabin staff propelled us all to the nearest seats. Faces taut with fear, hearts beating fast. The next explosion rocked the aircraft on its wheels. It was my three-year-old daughter who calmly pointed out the smoke rising from the tarmac a few feet from the left wing-tip. The third explosion was felt not heard. The sound was drowned by the roar of the jet engines, which were being started even as we were scrambling aboard. The captain swung the Boeing 707 onto the nearest runway and without stopping or taxi-ing to the end for maximum length the jet took off, banking and turning out to sea as soon as it was airborne.

A lucky escape. A brief item later on the BBC World Service news said that during an exchange of artillery fire some shells had landed on Beirut airport. The incident deserved no more; it was simply another in the long catalogue of violent acts that have scarred Lebanon for more than ten years. It was in itself insignificant; the airport had been shelled on numerous previous occasions and on this one, nobody was killed. The Lebanese have become used to daily violence on a scale that would horrify people in any other country in the world.

Our departure from Beirut that day was for a New Year break in Cyprus at the end of 1983. The shelling was part of an increasingly bloody conflict between Muslim militiamen on one side, and the Christian militiamen and mainly Christian units of the Lebanese Army on the other. Muslims against Christians – rather Muslim fighters against Christian fighters. That is the theme that runs through the history of modern Lebanon. Sometimes the conflict has been inflamed by outside powers, sometimes it has been suppressed by them, sometimes left to simmer unchecked. But in Lebanon you learn very quickly that little is exactly the way it looks

A description of the main religious groups, political organisations and leading personalities in the Lebanese Civil War forms part of this chapter on pp. 59–66.

45

at first sight. Leave aside the fighters, for example, and you will find Muslims and Christians working side by side, on occasions even living side by side. The depressing trend, however, is the other way: less communal integration and more polarisation. And as if the pattern is not already complicated enough, there have been a number of inter-Muslim and inter-Christian battles.

The problem is that Lebanon does not feel like a country as we know it in the West. It has all the external trappings, a flag, a constitution, a government, an army, and so on. But the first and most powerful allegiance of the Lebanese people – especially in times of trouble – is towards none of these symbols of nationhood; rather, it is to family and clan. Both are clustered around religious groups; hence the polarisation.

Like its neighbours, Lebanon is the creation of colonial powers, its borders defined by the pencils and rulers of the colonialists. This historical fact goes a long way towards explaining why Lebanon has had such difficulty in finding internal cohesion and why it is such a horrifying and perplexing mess today. Lebanon was never meant to be a country, and such attempts as there have been to make it one have come unstuck, partly because of the inherent contradictions and partly because it has suited Lebanon's neighbours to keep it weak and divided.

France was the dominant foreign influence in the creation of Lebanon, and French influence, direct and indirect, remains strong today. Most educated Lebanese speak French as a second language. Britain and France, after the end of the First World War, carved up the region, Britain taking Palestine, France taking Lebanon and Syria under its wing. Up till then, the whole region (present-day Israel, the occupied West Bank, Jordan, Syria and Lebanon) had been part of the Ottoman empire. And in the middle and later years of the last century there was already growing hostility between the Maronite Christian community and the Druze, leading to terrifying blood-letting, and prompting the French to intervene. (The Maronites still, more than any other Lebanese community, look to France for guidance and inspiration.) In 1920 the French created the state of Greater Lebanon, which encompassed nearly all of what is today known as Lebanon. Over the next twenty years a system of power-sharing emerged, with top jobs being distributed among the various religious groups, but with the Maronite Christians (then, but not now, the biggest single group) getting the lion's share of the power. Under the unwritten

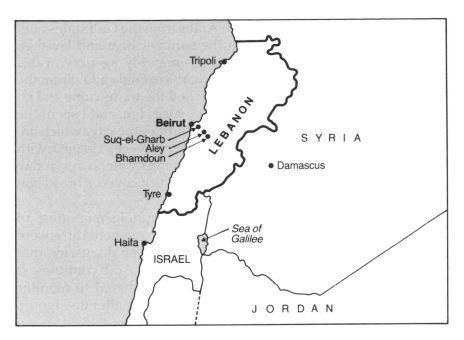

National Pact of 1943 the President of Lebanon is always a Maronite, the Prime Minister a Sunni Muslim, the speaker of the House of Representatives a Shiite Muslim, and so on. If one has to try to sum up what has been happening in Lebanon in recent years and explain it in the simplest way possible, then one could say that Muslims (now reckoned to be in the majority, although some Christians still deny this – the last census was conducted in 1932) are trying to win a more equitable share of power and the Christians are trying to hang on to what they have traditionally enjoyed. In years gone by, it was the Christians who were the best educated and the most powerful members of the community. Recent years have seen this pattern change: the Muslim community has grown fast, and Muslims have been receiving education and training sufficient to give them opportunities which had not been available in the past. This is particularly true of the Shiites, for decades the underdogs of Lebanese society, traditionally working in country areas. These days the Shiites (the biggest single group in the country) are flexing their muscles and demanding a fair share of the cake. In a nutshell, the Muslims want a redefining of the National Pact.

The memory that many people still have of Lebanon is of the days when it was the playground of the rich. The country where you could ski in the mountains and water-ski on the Mediter-

47

ranean on the same day; where rich Arabs from the Gulf states built villas in the mountains to escape the summer heat and lavished their money on the night-clubs and casinos. My memory of this period is only through the eyes of an eight-year old child. From the balcony of our house in rue Bliss I watched the trams come and go as my parents got involved in the hectic social life, and I spent the afternoons on the long sandy beaches south of the city, which are now choked with rubbish and washed with waves clogged with plastic bottles and untreated sewage. Arriving by air on a clear day you can look down on a carpet of rubbish which covers a broad belt of sea off the Lebanese coast.

Beirut in those pre-civil war days was the publishing house of the Arab world, the city whose French-style pavement cafés were the stage for political debate and the kind of open discussion that was increasingly being suppressed in the other Arab countries. It was the city where foreign correspondents gathered to monitor events in the region and where they came to relax after the rigours of their travels.

It is perhaps too easy to look back on this period through rose-coloured glasses because the cracks were in fact never very far from the surface. For example, in 1958 tension rose between Muslims, who favoured closer relations with Egypt and the pan-Arab policies of President Nasser, and Christians (led by President Chamoun), who pressed for closer ties with the United States. When the pro-Western monarchy was overthrown in Iraq in July 1958 (see p. 85), President Chamoun asked for US troops to be sent to Lebanon to preserve Lebanese independence. Some 10 000 were despatched, to be withdrawn a short time later, following a change of President in Lebanon and strong protests from the Soviet Union and China.

The biggest trouble, however, was yet to come. From the late 1960s until 1982, Palestinian activity in Lebanon was to play a major part in that country's destiny. As PLO guerrillas used Lebanon as a base for attacks against Israel, at the same time setting up what amounted to a state within a state, so the Israeli reprisals were stepped up (on one occasion in 1968 Israeli commandos destroyed thirteen airliners at Beirut airport). The expulsion of the Palestinians from Jordan in 1970 and 1971 led to the PLO becoming a major presence in Lebanon and exposed the weakness of the Lebanese army and government, which were unable to control or restrict their movements. In 1973 there were clashes between

Arabs from three regions of the Arab World. ABOVE *A young boy in the traditional galabiyya leads a donkey through a sandy street in Cairo, towards a van carrying Western soft drinks.* LEFT *The late King Khalid of Saudi Arabia symbolises the success of the oil boom.* RIGHT *Moroccan women old and young.*

LEFT   Gerald Butt in Arab dress, 1952. RIGHT   Gerald Butt, his sister and his parents by the Dead Sea, Jericho, 1952. BELOW   Gerald's father greets the young King Hussein on the latter's return to Amman from a trip abroad in August 1955.

Three men and two camels fill the centre of Abu Dhabi in 1958 where the first foreign bank, the British Bank of the Middle East, was shortly to be opened. LEFT   Gerald Butt at Amman Airport, Jordan 1953. RIGHT   Gerald Butt today, on a hill overlooking the walled city of Fez, Morocco, which houses the world's oldest university.

An Egyptian village stands between the edge of the desert and the Nile valley, near Luxor. BELOW *The skyline of present-day Riyadh.*

ABOVE *For a fare of 5p, a steamer ferries people across the Nile from Luxor to the 'Western Bank'. Three miles away into the countryside are the tombs of the Valley of the Kings and Valley of the Queens.*
LEFT *Fighters of the PLO prepare to leave Tripoli in north Lebanon at the end of 1983, forced out by fellow Palestinian fighters disillusioned with the leadership of Yasir Arafat.*

The Temple of Queen Hatshepsut near the Valley of the Kings (Thebes) built in c. 1500 BC and first examined by Napoleon's savants early last century. LEFT The rooftops of Cairo, the world's most crowded city. Estimates say that up to fifteen million people are packed into this city intended for a fraction of that number. Hundreds of thousands live in shanty towns.

LEFT   *President Sadat moments before his assassination at the annual military parade to commemorate the 1973 war with Israel; he is flanked by Egyptian Defence Minister and Vice-president Mubarak.* RIGHT   *Minutes later, after the attack by soldiers taking purl in the parade.* BELOW   *Adoring crowds welcome Gamal Abdul Nasser to Damiettu.*

A minaret rises high above the houses of this Tunisian city; from the covered balcony the muezzin *calls the faithful to prayer.*

Phalangists and Palestinians. The big Palestinian presence had upset the very delicate confessional balance in the country, and Christians felt that the government was not doing enough to curb their activities. In 1975, the tensions exploded into full-scale civil warfare which has never really ended – the PLO fighters backing Muslim and nationalist groups against the right-wing Christian militias.

Street-fighting and artillery duels engulfed the country, leaving large stretches of the capital in ruins, including the commercial heart of Beirut and the sea-front area where the big hotels (including the famous and most luxurious of all, the St George's) were located. They still stand empty today – gutted, charred and ghostly towers; and peace has never lasted long enough to allow the commercial districts to be rebuilt. The civil war saw the creation of the inappropriately named Green Line – a strip of bleak and frightening urban wasteland ravaged by war that divides the city between the predominantly Muslim west and the Christian east. In Arabic it is known simply as the 'confrontation line', which is a much more accurate description. For, apart from brief periods, this 'line' has been in existence ever since 1975, a physical manifestation of a mental attitude that sadly is becoming more, not less pronounced in the Lebanese.

The other major development in the civil fighting which has left an estimated 60 000 people dead and many more than that injured, was the intervention of Syria. The Syrian army intervened when the Christians looked threatened by the combined forces of left-wing, Muslim and Palestinian fighters, in an attempt to end the war. Fierce battles developed between the Syrians and the Palestinians, sowing the seeds of hatred which were to blossom in the subsequent years. An Arab League force was set up to keep the peace, but it was short-lived – soon to consist only of Syrians. Syrian troops have been in Lebanon ever since, deployed (these days some 40 000 of them) in the north and east of the country. Many Lebanese take the view (and it's the fear of many Christians) that it is Syria's ultimate desire to set up a 'Greater Syria', incorporating Lebanon and Jordan (the pre-colonial boundaries) into its own territory, and that, therefore, it has no intention of pulling its troops out of Lebanon.

If Syria has been one strong influence on Lebanon, the other has been the second 'regional super-power', Israel. The Lebanese people often say that if they were left alone, if all the foreign forces left, then there would be no more problems. This, unfortunately, is almost certainly wishful thinking, and probably equally certainly will never be put to the test. For it is undeniably true that Lebanon has found itself being used like a whore in the scramble for regional and international influence. Its cities and villages have been abused and despoiled in recent years by Syrian, Israeli and American armaments as much as, or even more than, they have been by Lebanese fighting Lebanese.

The Israeli involvement in Lebanon was prompted by the presence of PLO fighters there. PLO raids on Israeli targets prompted swift and harsh retaliation (see p. 74). In 1978 the Israelis invaded southern Lebanon, killing not only Palestinians but many Lebanese villagers. Under United States pressure they agreed to pull back, and a United Nations Interim Force (UNIFIL) was deployed to supervise and ensure the withdrawal. But with the Israelis' habitual contempt for UN resolutions, UNIFIL has never been able to fulfil its mandate; Israel has held on to a strip of Lebanese territory close to the border which is patrolled by its troops and its client Lebanese militia, the South Lebanon Army. Furthermore Israel has constantly harassed the UNIFIL forces, in an effort to discredit them and force them to leave. Towards the end of 1986 UNIFIL troops sustained a number of deaths and injuries at the hands of militiamen belonging to the pro-Iranian group, Hizbollah. Again UNIFIL called on Israel to pull back to the border as required by the terms of UN resolutions, but once more Israel refused.

The next major incursion was the invasion of June 1982. The details – the siege of Beirut, the eventual departure of the 8000 PLO fighters and the subsequent massacres of Palestinians in the Sabra and Chatila camps are described in Chapter 5 'The Palestinians'. The aftermath of the massacres saw the start of an era of strong Western, and especially American, influence in Lebanon's affairs. American marines took up positions at Beirut airport, an Italian contingent was deployed around the Palestinian camps, the French patrolled the city, and a tiny British contingent (joining after all the rest) set up home in a deserted tobacco factory in a largely derelict area to the south of the city, a stone's throw from an Israeli army forward position. The whole unit was known as the Multi-National Force (MNF).·

Brave messages of support for the new Lebanese leader Amin Gemayel (brother of Bashir, who was assassinated in September

1982 in a car-bomb attack) poured out of Washington; President Gemayel was received with great pomp in the White House. And to underline the support, American military equipment was sent to Lebanon and US officers were sent to retrain and rebuild the army which had been discredited during the civil war of the mid-seventies when it split along sectarian lines. This venture, like the whole American involvement in Lebanon, was to turn out to be disastrously unrealistic. But the crunch did not come right away.

There was, in fact, a honeymoon period of a few months when an air of optimism replaced the gloom of the preceding years. There was talk of reconstruction and political reconciliation. President Gemayel announced the elimination of the Green Line, and to prove the point made several visits to the mainly Muslim West Beirut – something presidents had rarely done in the past. During this period it was possible to travel at night to restaurants all over the city and in mountain areas which for years had been inaccessible to one community or another.

On 18 April 1983, it all started to go wrong. On that dark and thundery day I was just leaving the office to go to lunch with friends when I heard a sound which in the following months was to become familiar; the body-shaking roar of a car-bomb explosion. I grabbed a tape recorder and ran in the direction of the blast. It was further away than I imagined. I kept running through the lines of blocked traffic with radios in each car already beginning to blare out news flashes. 'Where's the explosion?' I asked one driver. 'As-Sifara al-Amrikiya.' The American Embassy. Right down on the seafront. Before I got there I could see and smell the smoke, and hear the sirens. When I arrived I could not believe what I was see-ing. Bodies, charred and mutilated were being carried out of the smoking ruins – some were walking, their clothes torn, their faces carrying looks of frozen horror; a black US Marine was standing on a pile of debris brandishing his gun in the pretence that he still had something to protect. For the embassy building was wrecked. A vehicle packed with explosives had rammed into the entrance, bringing down the building above. The front of the embassy had simply disappeared; the floors further inside had pancaked downwards like concrete playing cards, one overlapping the next. Hours after the blast a body could still be seen hanging upside-down, trapped between two of these upper floors.

I was to see worse carnage in the months ahead, but none had such an impact on me as this first suicide blast. It spelt the end of the honeymoon, and it was the beginning of the end of American involvement in Lebanon. The next decisive step happened a month later. During this time, under pressure from the United States, Lebanon and Israel had talks aimed at securing the withdrawal of the Israeli army from Lebanon, and on 17 May it was signed. The agreement was met with anger by many Muslim groups (and some Christians) and by the Syrians, who felt that it was tantamount to a peace treaty with Israel and would serve only American and Israeli interests. A National Salvation Front was set up to oppose the Gemayel administration and the government of Chafic Wazzan. In the following months, clashes between Muslim and Christian militias intensified, and the Lebanese army was ordered on a number of occasions to shell Shiite suburbs of Beirut, orders which were eventually to split the army once more.

A prelude to the troubles ahead came in August 1983 with fierce battles on the streets of West Beirut between the army and Muslim militiamen. For once the Lebanese army went into action in a big way. With guidance from American officers who were in Beirut to advise and re-train the army, the troops went on a ferocious mopping-up campaign to clear the streets of gunmen, inflicting heavy damage and considerable loss of life. Families sheltered as best they could in the stair-wells and basements of blocks of flats as the tanks blasted sniper positions on the roof-tops and balconies. In a sense the action of the army, accompanied by optimistic assessments from the American advisers of its capabilities, gave a false sense of hope that it might, against all the odds, be a body to be respected. But the American assessment of the Lebanese army was as far from the mark as its assessment of the whole Lebanese scene, failing to take into account the underlying politicial pressures. As the weeks went by there were more and more attacks on the army; the pressure mounted and the cracks began to show.

In September 1983 the clashes escalated into full-scale fighting in the Chouf mountains to the east and south-east of Beirut, following the sudden withdrawal of the Israeli army from these areas. Christian militiamen of the Lebanese Forces had entered the Chouf (a traditional Druze area) on the tails of the Israeli army the previous year. The Druze inflicted heavy defeats on the Lebanese Forces and drove them out. Lebanese army positions also came under attack – the army in the minds of the Druze being a tool of the Gemayel administration. Much of the fighting centred on the strategic hill-top town of Suq el-Gharb which is the last protection for the presidential palace. To reach the front-line involved a hazardous drive up an exposed hill-side. In a deserted hotel where once tourists admired the view of Beirut, exhausted Lebanese troops grabbed what rest they could between bouts of heavy shelling from Druze positions in Aley and Bhamdoun. The destruction of the buildings, streets and vehicles was matched by the squalor inside the hotel – the smell of rotting food and human excrement.

I drove back from one such visit with my colleague Keith Graves. We had reached what we thought was the safety of the city when there was a colossal explosion about a 100 yards ahead of us – not just one explosion in fact, but hundreds. A shell had landed on the ammunition dump of the Italian contingent of the Multi-National Force. We took shelter in the nearest building, which shook as rounds set off by the fire whizzed dangerously in all directions.

Life for the Multi-National Force had been becoming more dangerous in every way. With the exception of the French, the various contingents, especially the Americans, bunkered down. They clearly could not perform any useful role. The US marine headquarters at the airport came under frequent attack, and the marines returned fire. Eventually the US Fleet were called into use, with the big guns of the mighty battleship *New Jersey* rocking the city as it pounded positions in the mountains, at times to halt attacks on the marines, at other times in support of the increasingly strained Lebanese army. My strong memory of this period is of the sound of shelling, the sound of the guns of the big ships and the whine of US fighter jets as they wheeled over the capital. On a Sunday morning in October we were awoken early by another distant boom; the second, which followed a short time later, we did not hear. The first turned out to be a suicide attack on a French MNF building on the edge of West Beirut (58 men dead), the second on the US marine headquarters further south at the airport (241 men dead). This disastrous chapter in American foreign policy was brought to a sudden close. Overnight, with the American presidential elections coming up, the memory of what had happened in Lebanon was swept under the carpet. It suddenly became a subject that Americans chose not to think about, and the US ceased to have a Lebanon policy. Many of the men who served there are bitter. Marine Corporal Michael Petit, who's now out of the service, has put down his recollections in a book; and he concludes: '. . . the marines had accomplished nothing in Lebanon except a senseless loss of life.' In my view he was right.

By the end of February 1984, all the MNF troops with the exception of the French had been withdrawn from Lebanon. What finally nudged them out was what happened on 6 February, a date which no-one who was in Beirut at the time will ever forget.

The Lebanese government had been coming under increasing political pressure because of the troop withdrawal agreement signed with Israel, while the army was coming under military strain. There was growing anger among Muslim officers in the army at the way they were being ordered to shell Muslim areas. Eventually, the Shiite leader, Nabih Berri, ordered Shiite officers to disobey such commands. This they did. On 5 February the government resigned.

Living in Lebanon, you learn to trust your instincts. On Monday 6 February I made the mistake of not being guided by my own. There was an unmistakable atmosphere of tension on the streets that morning. Something was in the air. The schools stayed closed as they do whenever there is trouble expected. My wife and I discussed whether this was the moment that she and the two girls should leave. We decided to give it one more day. I went to the office. An hour or so later, gunmen came onto the streets, the army ordered an immediate curfew with the threat that anyone breaking it would be shot. The army had finally split – Shiite brigades teaming up with Muslim militiamen who'd taken over control of Muslim West Beirut. My family was trapped in our flat a mile or two away. As I made contact with London, my colleague Chris Drake drove off, returning later with the family, having driven at break-neck speed through the anarchy and pandemonium of West Beirut. As they reached the safety of the Commodore Hotel, the shelling started, with units of the army loyal to the President and Christian militiamen pounding the west of the city. My family spent the next two days sheltering in the basement of the hotel while the city rocked around us. Two days after that they and much of the rest of the foreign community were evacuated by British and American military helicopters to Cyprus.

The time since then has been dominated by more muscle-flexing by the Muslim community and growing Syrian involvement in Lebanese affairs. The fall of the Wazzan government and the collapse of the Lebanese army marked the end of American and Israeli efforts to set up a government of their liking in Beirut. Indeed, under pressure from Syria and Muslim leaders President Gemayel had no choice but to abrogate the troop withdrawal agreement signed by him a year earlier. Much of the energy of the Shiite Muslim community was then directed at the Israeli army which, despite a partial pull-back, was still occupying a sizeable area of southern Lebanon. Shiite villagers, motivated and fortified in courage by their faith in Islam carried out dozens of attacks on the Israelis, inflicting casualties at a rate which prompted adverse public opinion at home. It was the first time that the powerful Israeli military machine had suffered such humiliation – and at the hands of what Professor Kemal Salibi of the American University of Beirut has called 'a classic peasants' revolt'. The Shiites, tired of the role of underdog, had been prepared to fight and die for their freedom. Religion (inspired by the Islamic revolution in Iran) was an energising factor; but this was not, as many people chose to see it, an explosion of Muslim fundamentalism.

It's left to the Syrians now to try to cement together this crumbling nation and they have tried many times. Most of the top political leaders (though, significantly, not all the militia leaders, those who hold the real power in Lebanon) were persuaded to attend a conference of 'National Reconciliation' in Geneva in October 1983; no progress was made. After the collapse of the Wazzan government and the abrogation of the troop withdrawal agreement of 17 May 1983 the same leaders were gathered in a luxury hotel in Lausanne. But little happened that could be construed as progress in bringing the various opposing factions closer together. Indeed, fresh differences emerged among the mainly Muslim bloc which had been formed to bring down the Wazzan administration. And on the key question of political reforms to give the Muslim community more representation in running Lebanon no headway whatsoever was made.

Since then the Syrians have been wrestling with this very problem; and despite their close geographical and sociological ties with Lebanon they have been finding life as hard as every other foreign power which has tried to intervene in Lebanese affairs. The Israeli Defence Minister, Mr Yitzhak Rabin, speaking towards the end of 1984, said: 'We all learn the hard way. Whoever sets his foot in Lebanon sinks in the Lebanese quagmire. We want to be out of it.' How often those sentiments must have been expressed over the years.

Muslim political and militia leaders are summoned frequently to Damascus for talks with the vice-president who has been assigned the thankless task of trying to sort out Lebanon, Mr Abdel-Halim

Khaddam. (Diplomats in Damascus who've been following developments over the years say he's looking increasingly weary. Little wonder.) In the end, what are needed are wide-ranging political reforms, but in the short term much of the effort is directed at bringing to an end the internecine fighting and general lawlessness in predominantly Muslim West Beirut. Numerous security plans are announced with great fanfare in Damascus. But their progress is sadly predictable: they all start with promise and for a few days the gunmen disappear from the streets; the militia offices close; and the militia flags are put away. The artillery which flanks the Green Line is silent. The Lebanese army sets up checkpoints and searches cars for weapons. But you don't have to be a cynic to predict what will happen. Gradually the gunmen reappear, the army melts away and lawlessness returns. Quite simply the army, which has been discredited so often, does not command the respect of the population, and the central government has no authority.

At the end of 1985 hopes were raised when a package of reforms to give Muslims a greater say in Lebanon was drawn up and signed – not, this time, by the traditional warlords, but by the younger generation of militia leaders, the men who command the gunmen on the streets. But hopes once again were short-lived. The Christian community as a whole refused to accept the agreement, believing that it was a sell-out of already dwindling Christian interests and a surrendering of Lebanon's national rights to Syria. The man who signed for the Christians, the leader of the Lebanese Forces militia, Mr Elie Hobeika, was forced to flee following fierce street battles. Among those who rejected the Syrian plan was President Gemayel. This won him badly needed support within his own community which had earlier accused him of surrendering to Syrian pressure.

In 1986 the state of affairs in West Beirut became so bad that, for the first time since the Israeli invasion of 1982, the Syrians sent a number of their own officers into the city to supervise the latest security plan. For a time this plan seemed to be working better than previous ones. But it didn't stop the violence. The kidnappings of Lebanese and foreigners continued; so did the fighting across the Green Line. Furthermore the number of robberies rose sharply as the economic slump worsened and the value of the pound – once one of the strongest currencies in the region – plummeted. The car-bombing continued too, in particular in East Beirut. The Christians blamed the Syrians and their Lebanese allies. They believed the bombings were aimed at forcing the Christians to accept the Syrian reform plan as signed by Mr Hobeika, an impression which was reinforced when Mr Hobeika and his supporters, backed by Muslim militiamen, tried to storm East Beirut from the west of the city in the autumn of 1986.

Frightened by the violence and, in particular, by the kidnappings, most foreigners have left Lebanon (or certainly at least West Beirut where most of the embassies and foreign firms used to be based). At the time of writing about 25 foreigners are missing, believed kidnapped. Five Americans and three Frenchmen are being held by Islamic Jihad, a group about which very little is known. It's believed to be made up of Shiite extremists linked in some way to Iran who are demanding the release from prison in Kuwait of 17 Arabs for bomb attacks against American and French targets there in 1983. Kuwait is adamant that there will never be a deal.

Incidents like these mean much more, of course, when you know the individuals involved. Another day in Beirut that I will never forget is a particular Saturday in March 1985. Don Mell, a photographer from the Associated Press rushed into our office. 'They've taken Terry,' he said – we went numb with disbelief and fear. He'd been with Terry Anderson, the AP bureau chief, when gunmen forced him out of a car and drove him away. The two men had just been playing tennis. Terry has not been seen since, though he has communicated by letter and a video-taped appeal to the American government was released in 1986.

Around Christmas time in 1985 the special envoy of the Archbishop of Canterbury, Mr Terry Waite, made what has so far been his last attempt in Beirut to secure the release of the kidnapped Americans. But whatever progress may have been made then, the American bombing of Libya the following year wiped it out. The US raid and Britain's support for it led to the murder of two British teachers who'd been kidnapped previously and the abduction of a third. Foreign teachers from the American University of Beirut (AUB), once one of the most highly respected institutions in the Middle East, left en masse. The AUB had found itself in the middle of a war zone for a decade, but for most of this time it remained a haven of sanity, a platform where political and confessional differences were buried in the interests of academic achievement. It was quite literally an oasis – a campus of fine stone buildings set among lawns and colourful flower beds, shaded by tall trees. It was here that we would bring our children to play. Stepping into the campus was to step out of the concrete nightmare of West Beirut and away from the threat of violence. The motto over the gate of the AUB reads: 'That they may have life and have it more abundantly.' The forlorn wish of the ordinary Lebanese people.

Tens of thousands of Lebanese have given up. The violence, the disruption of education and the very severe economic crisis have forced many of the families who can afford it to look for a new life abroad. Tens of thousands of Lebanese died without even having that choice.

For those left behind these are depressing days. The famous 'Lebanese resilence' which everyone used to talk about has finally been used up. The beauty of some of the scenery is about all the country can boast – that and the restaurants which, despite the problems, still produce the finest food and the most imaginative cuisine in the Levant.

Much more on the minds of the Lebanese than the physical scars and deteriorating public services (lengthy and irregular power cuts, a crippled telephone service, filthy streets) are the mental scars. The worry of living every day in danger. The first thought that flashes through your mind when you hear an explosion or shooting is: where is the family? Are they safe? Abed lost the aunt who had been a mother to him in one of the huge car bombs in the southern suburbs. The shock made his wife give birth prematurely. No one knows who planted the bomb and why they chose a crowded residential area to detonate it. Nobody ever knows these things. It's all part of the fear and futility. People spend hours listening to local radio stations which broadcast news flashes every time there's trouble of any kind. Many of the reports are unreliable, but the Lebanese, voracious consumers of news, listen all the same.

And what of the next generation? One mother told me of how her teenage children show no respect for any kind of authority. 'How can you expect anything else,' she said, 'when their friends are in militias, when they see every law in the country, even about parking and driving, ignored by the vast majority of people, where taxes are never collected, when the schools are closed for weeks on end because of the shelling?' One evening at her house one of her sons was insisting, against his parents' wishes, on going out for the evening even though there had been shelling all day. 'I've survived ten years of shelling, so what the hell'. One Lebanese doctor defined this attitude for me as: 'Fatalism with a capital F.'

The family is still the central unit in Lebanon, as in all Arab countries. And the extended family provides the social security cover that individuals need. But because of deaths, kidnappings, forced separations as thousands of people become refugees from the fighting (on some occasions for the second or third time) or travel abroad, the home-made welfare system has begun to creak under the strain.

How deep the scars of forced uprootings and separations go will become clear only when Lebanon can enjoy a tranquil period again and society can examine the damage inflicted on it. There will be no shortage of evidence to look at. The child's drawing I saw of a tank firing and a shell impacting against a high-rise building was painted with the chilling realism, clarity and horror that only someone who'd seen such a thing could have portrayed. Then there's the boy who saw his father die when their house got hit by a shell. He goes to school each day on the bus with the other boys. But he doesn't join in the class. He stays in a room on his own, curled up on a mattress, silent. And then there's the student who's reported by his teacher to be tired and inattentive in class because by night he fights for the local militia. How much will family life, and indeed Lebanon itself, mean to them in the future?

The Five Main Religious Groups

Christians

Maronites   Named after a fifth-century recluse, this sect emerged in the seventh century and is today the biggest single group in the Christian community. Since 1180 it has been linked to the Roman Catholic Church but has been allowed to keep its own rites, Syriac liturgy and religious practices. It has a long history of conflict with the *Druze*, both sides having carried out massacres of each other's followers. The Maronites are aware that they are a small minority group in a predominantly Muslim area, and many feel aggrieved that Christian (and especially European) countries do not do more to support them in the face of increasing Muslim power and influence in Lebanon. This fear of an Islamic takeover has given the Maronites a siege mentality. Under the unwritten National Covenant of 1943, the President of Lebanon is a Maronite, and members of the same community hold other key posts.

Greek Orthodox and Greek Catholic   As a group they are not allocated any of the top jobs in the country, reflecting the small size of the community.

Muslims

Druze   The origins of this mystical sect are uncertain, but it is an off-shoot of one of the minority Shiia sects of the twelfth century, and many Muslims believe that the Druze faith is not part of Islam. The Druze people have a reputation for being very tough fighters and for the past century have been involved in bloody clashes with the *Maronites*, and massacres have been committed by both communities. The Druze have been fighting with other Muslims to pressure the Maronites to give up some of the power they have traditionally enjoyed.

Shiia   In the seventh century, some thirty years after the death of the Prophet Muhammad, a major split occurred in Islam over the succession of the leadership, and the Shiites broke away from the *Sunni* majority. In Lebanon, the Shiites were traditionally the underdogs of society, being on the whole uneducated and working on the land. But times have changed: they are now the biggest single group in the country and many of them hold top business and academic posts. The Shiite Muslim revolution in Iran gave impetus to a desire for a change in the way the top jobs in the government and army in Lebanon were allocated, and the Shiites joined with the *Druze* in battles against the *Maronites* to pressure them to relinquish some of their power. At the moment the speaker of Parliament is, under the unwritten National Pact of 1943, a Shiite. The Shiite community is concentrated in southern Lebanon, Beirut and the Bekaa valley.

Sunni   The vast majority of Muslims in the world are Sunnis, and therefore they are considered 'orthodox'. In Lebanon they have traditionally been the traders, with powerful communities in the port cities of Beirut, Tripoli and Sidon. Under the unwritten National Pact of 1943 the Prime Minister is a Sunni. In recent years, many Sunnis in Lebanon have felt that they are in danger of losing out to the other groups, most of whom have powerful militias to back up their claims for more power and territory.

The Organisations

Amal (the Arabic for 'hope') The major political and military organisation representing the interests of the Shiite Muslim community headed since 1980 by *Nabih Berri*. Founded by Shiite spiritual leader Imam Musa Sadr, a charismatic leader who went missing in Libya in 1980. Lebanese Shiites accuse the Libyans of holding him and have hijacked a number of planes demanding his release. Libya denies the charge. Photographs of the Imam, alongside those of Ayatollah Khomeni of Iran, can frequently be seen hung together in Shiite areas of Lebanon. The Amal militia played a major part in the overthrow of the Lebanese army in Muslim West Beirut in February 1984 and is now the dominant militia in that half of the city. While Amal has majority Shiite support, it has come under pressure from more radical groups (*Islamic Amal* and *Hizbollah* which have close links with Iran) to pursue more radical Islamic policies. In 1985, Amal failed to take over three Palestinian refugee camps in Beirut, being forced back by heavy Palestinian resistance. The *Progressive Socialist Party* sided with the Palestinians, and this was part of the cause of heavy fighting between the two supposed allies later that year. Amal is believed to have some 6000 full-time fighters, but claims an irregular force of more than 12 000.

Lebanese Forces The main fighting force in the Christian community, it came into being during the Lebanese civil war in the mid-seventies, bringing together four right-wing Christian militias. Its members are mostly *Maronites* and it is seen as the military wing of the *Phalange Party*, although at times it has been at considerable odds with the party. The Lebanese Forces received support from Israel and when the Israelis invaded Lebanon in 1982 they went with the invading army into Druze areas of the Chouf mountains. After the sudden withdrawal of the Israelis in autumn 1983 the Lebanese Forces were soundly beaten by the *Progressive Socialist Party*. Later they were forced to withdraw from areas they'd held in southern Lebanon, following further Israeli pullouts. The Lebanese Forces have always refused to be represented in cabinet, unlike the other main militias. In 1985 a rebellion inside the militia caused a major rift with the Phalange Party. Later that year the leader at the time, Mr Elie Hobeika, signed a political and security agreement with Syria on behalf of the Christian community. The agreement was bitterly opposed by the community and, after heavy fighting, Mr Hobeika was forced to leave the country. In October 1986 Mr Hobeika and his supporters, backed by Muslim militiamen, tried to seize power in East Beirut in an attack from the west of the city. After fierce fighting and the intervention of Lebanese troops the Lebanese Forces pushed them back.

The Murabitoun (in English 'the garrisoned troops') The militia of the *Sunni* Muslim community, a power during the Lebanese civil war and for some years after. But they were as good as wiped out and their radio was shut down in street battles in 1985 with *Amal* militiamen who accused them of plotting with Palestinian fighters to work together to become a major force in Muslim West Beirut. This has meant that the Sunni community has been excluded from inter-militia talks on the future of Lebanon.

National Liberal Party (NLP) A small party within the *Maronite* Christian community founded in 1958 by supporters of *Camille Chamoun*. It forms part of the Lebanese Front, a coalition of Christian groups dominated by the *Phalange Party*.

The Phalange Party (in Arabic *al-Kata'eb*) The dominant political party representing the interests of the *Maronite* Christian community. Founded in 1936 by Pierre Gemayel under the influence of the nationalist movement in Germany at that time, following a visit to Berlin. The Phalangists have tried to maintain friendly, if distant, relations with Syria, but have generally looked to the West and Israel for support.

Progressive Socialist Party (PSP) Led by *Walid Jumblatt*, it represents the interests of the *Druze* community, although it has some members from other communities. It controls the Chouf mountains east and south east of Beirut, having driven out the *Lebanese Forces* after fierce fighting in autumn 1983. It was part of the opposition bloc which brought down the Wazzan government early in 1984, and which in turn precipitated the disintegration of the Lebanese army and the takeover of Beirut by PSP and *Amal*. While those two are nominal allies (both backed by Syria) they have been involved in heavy street fighting between themselves, notably in 1985. The Druze also have a rather ambiguous relationship with the Israelis because of the presence of a Druze community in Israel.

PSP is reckoned to have some 6000 regular fighters and the same number of reservists. It has received Soviet-made tanks and other equipment from Libya.

Among the other groups

Hizbollah (meaning 'Party of God') An off-shoot of *Amal*, a fundamentalist *Shiite* Muslim group with strong spiritual and financial connections with Iran. It has no more than a few hundred militiamen and is led by fundamentalist sheikhs. While there is no proof, members of Hizbollah are thought to have been involved in a number of suicide attacks against Western targets in Lebanon. Its leader is believed to be Sheikh Muhammed Hussein Fadlallah. By the end of 1986 there were signs of strain between Hizbollah and Amal, with Hizbollah challenging Amal's previously undisputed authority in southern Lebanon. Hizbollah carried out attacks against troops of the United Nations force UNIFIL and the *South Lebanon Army*.

Islamic Amal Another fundamentalist Iranian-influenced off-shoot of *Amal*, centred on Baalbeck in the Bekaa valley. Led by Hussein Musawi, it has mustered only a few hundred fighters.

Lebanese Communist Party Urges closer co-operation with the Soviet Union and supports anti-American moves in the region. Its leader, George Hawi, is a *Greek Orthodox*.

Marada (meaning 'giants') A Christian militia led by former President *Suleiman Franjieh*. Estimates put the force at around 5000 men.

Syrian Social Nationalist Party (SSNP) As the name suggests, a party with strong links with Syria. It is strongest in northern Lebanon, and is multi-confessional with a big Christian (*Maronite* and *Greek Orthodox*) element. The party advocates the creation of 'Greater Syria', which would include Syria, Lebanon, Jordan, present-day Israel and Cyprus. It has its own militia, and its members have carried out suicide car-bomb attacks against the Israeli army in southern Lebanon.

Palestine Liberation Organisation (PLO) Although the PLO was forced out of Beirut in 1982 following the Israeli invasion, many fighters have returned to northern and eastern Lebanon (and some, according to reports, to Beirut). There are estimated to be about 5000 in the country at the moment split between supporters of the PLO Chairman, Mr Yasir Arafat, and PLO dissidents backed by Syria. There is strong support for the PLO in the refugee camps near Tyre and Sidon in southern Lebanon. PLO positions and headquarters in these camps were the target of frequent Israeli air raids in 1986.

Popular Liberation Army   A loose alliance of *Shiites, Sunnis* and *Druze* in southern Lebanon which has been attacking the occupying Israeli army and its client militias.

South Lebanon Army (SLA)   A predominantly Christian force trained and armed by Israel to maintain security (with Israeli help) in a strip of territory which runs along Lebanon's border with Israel. It was founded by a deserter from the Lebanese army, Major Saad Haddad, in 1976. It is now run by a retired Lebanese army officer, General Antoine Lahad. The force contains an estimated 1500 men.

Leading Personalities:

Nabih Berri   Leader of the main *Shiite* Muslim militia and political organisation *Amal*. A middle-class lawyer who has family links with the United States. Minister with responsibility for southern Lebanon in the Karami cabinet. His militia played a leading part in the fighting which defeated the Lebanese army in Beirut in February 1984. A political ally of Syria, he was the chief mediator for the release of American hostages from a TWA airliner hijacked to Beirut in 1985.

Camille Chamoun   *Maronite* Christian. Former president and one of the old generation of Lebanese warlords. One of the founders and the former leader of the National Liberal Party (NLP) which advocates strong links with Western countries and opposes the idea of a Syrian-dominated Lebanon. His son Dany is now leader of the party. The NLP is without a significant militia, as it was wiped out by the Christian *Lebanese Forces* in 1980.

Suleiman Franjieh   *Maronite* Christian. Former President and another of the older generation of Lebanese warlords, but now something of an exile from the heart of the Maronite Christian community, living in northern Lebanon near Tripoli. Strong ally of Syria and very critical of the *Phalangist Party's* links with Israel, and of its influence over the running of Lebanon. The split with his Maronite colleagues was completed in 1978 when his son, Tony, and his wife and daughter were killed after a family palace was attacked by the *Lebanese Forces*. He has his own militia, the *Marada* brigades.

Dr Samir Geagea *Maronite* Christian. Leader of the *Lebanese Forces* militia. He led a revolt in the militia in 1985, accusing the *Phalangist Party* of having too close links with Syria. In 1986 he led a revolt against the *Lebanese Forces'* leader at the time, Mr Elie Hobeika, who had signed a political and security agreement in Damascus on behalf of the Christian community which was fiercely opposed by it. Mr Hobeika was forced to leave Lebanon. Dr Geagea is a young man with a single-minded, some would say fanatical, belief in his cause and a spartan life-style.

Amin Gemayel *Maronite* Christian. President of Lebanon since September 1982, when his brother Bashir (who had recently been elected President) was assassinated. Lawyer and businessman, he is the son of Pierre Gemayel, one of the founders of the *Phalangist Party*. On taking office he looked to the West, and especially to the United States for support. (US Marines were part of a Multi-National Force stationed in Beirut at the time.) With US encouragement and with Christian support he signed an agreement on 17 May 1983 with Israel for the withdrawal of Israeli forces. This met with bitter hostility from Syria and Lebanese Muslims. A year later President Gemayel had no choice but to abrogate it. Then followed a period of close ties with Syria and worsening relations with his fellow Christians. This was reversed early in 1986 when he refused to endorse a Syrian-brokered political and security agreement for Lebanon (cf. *Dr Samir Geagea*).

Rashid Karami A *Sunni* Muslim from Tripoli in northern Lebanon. A lawyer by training, he has been Prime Minister on three occasions, the first being in 1955. He is one of the most solid pillars in the Lebanese political establishment, but lacks the militia support of some of his colleagues in the same position. He enjoys a close relationship with Syria, and the Syrians had a hand in appointing him head of the so-called government of National Reconciliation in 1984.

Walid Jumblatt   Druze chieftain. Head of one of the two leading Druze clans in Lebanon, he took over leadership of the community after the assassination of his father, Kemal Jumblatt, in 1977. Syrians were widely believed to have been behind the assassination, but Walid Jumblatt now enjoys Syrians' support. He is one of the most fiery, eccentric and outspoken figures on the Lebanese political scene. He is vocal in his condemnation of the *Phalangist Party* and the control it has over top Lebanese affairs. His militia, the *Progressive Socialist Party*, has played a major part in joint Muslim military efforts to pressure the Christian community to accept political change. He is a collector of guns which are displayed in his ancestral castle in Mukhtara in the Chouf mountains, an area now under what amounts to semi-autonomous Druze control.

5 *The Palestinians*

A people in search of a home

On a hot August day in 1982, 8000 fighters belonging to the Palestine Liberation Organisation (PLO) began leaving Beirut. They were being forced out, having earlier been driven out of their bases in southern Lebanon and having withstood, for two-and-a-half months, assaults from the land, sea and air by the Israeli armed forces, which culminated in the Israelis laying siege to the western half of Beirut. As Israeli planes and heavy armour pulverised certain quarters of West Beirut, the ground troops blocking its entrance prevented water and other essentials reaching those of us living inside. The PLO said they were pulling out to avoid further suffering to the civilian population of Beirut.

As the convoy of lorries threaded its way slowly through the devastated streets of the Lebanese capital, the fighters and their supporters fired their weapons into the air. The cacophony was ear-splitting. They fired everything they had, pistols, machine guns, rocket-propelled grenades, and even anti-aircraft guns. I found myself in one of the narrow streets lined with wrecked and gutted buildings leading down to Beirut port which had been the scene of fighting for many years. I crouched round the side of a hut to avoid being hit by falling bullets. (Several people were killed that way as the fighters left.) And over the roar of the guns I recorded my impressions on my tape recorder. I remember saying something to the effect that this would be the last time that PLO guns would be fired in Lebanon, as the fighters boarded ships that were to take them to several corners of the Arab world.

I was wrong. Just before Christmas in 1983, on a cold quayside in the northern Lebanese port city of Tripoli, I witnessed similar scenes. The PLO fighters were again being forced out, not, this time, by the Israelis, but by fellow Palestinian fighters disillusioned with the leadership of the PLO Chairman, Mr Yasir Arafat.

On both occasions, the firing into the air was intended as an act of defiance, to show that the PLO had not been beaten. On neither occasion was the argument convincing. For the truth is that the Palestine Liberation Organisation has not succeeded in liberating a square inch of occupied Arab land, and these two evacuations represented two more steps backward, two more steps further away from the Palestinian homeland. One by one, Arab states have chosen to distance themselves from the activities of the PLO, both military and political, sometimes fearing Israeli reprisals (Jordan is an example), sometimes wishing to avoid the threat to internal stability represented by the presence of a politically active and independent Palestinian community, and sometimes through frustration at an inability to control the Palestinian movement (for example, Syria). In short, the Palestinian movement in all its forms has few friends in the Arab world, regardless of what you might hear from the official propaganda of almost every Arab state.

There are reckoned to be over four million Palestinians in the world, half of whom are registered as refugees. Palestine as a country ceased to exist in May 1948 when the State of Israel was created (see map opposite). Since 1922 it had been a British mandate, but foreshadowings of the creation of a Jewish state in Palestine had come even before that. The Palestinians rate 2 November 1917 as one of the blackest days in their history. On that day the British Foreign Secretary at the time, Arthur James Balfour, wrote a letter to a prominent British Jew, Lord Rothschild. It became known as the Balfour Declaration.

All around the Arab world today, decades after the appearance of the Balfour Declaration and decades after the creation of the State of Israel, Arabs still remember. I don't think it is fully appreciated in Britain how much the Palestinians blame British governments from the days of Balfour onwards for what has happened to create the Palestinian problem. The Declaration itself is so often referred to and so seldom actually quoted that it is worth doing so here:

> 'His Majesty's Government view with favour the establishment in Palestine of a national home for the Jewish people, and will use their best endeavours to facilitate the achievement of this object, it being clearly understood that nothing shall be done which may prejudice the existing civil and religious rights of existing non-Jewish communities in Palestine or the rights and political status of Jews in other countries.'

The movement of Jews into Palestine at the eastern end of the Mediterranean had begun in the previous century. For the most part they were escaping from persecution in Russia and eastern European countries to return to that part of the world – the Bible

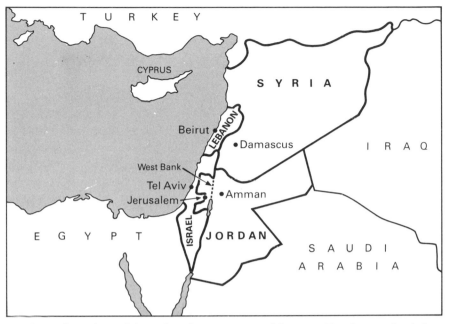

lands – that they felt to be their spiritual home. By the end of the
century Jewish leaders in Europe were talking about the possibility
of creating a country as a Jewish homeland, and the Zionist
movement was being born. In the decades after the Balfour Declaration, Jewish immigration to Palestine continued, despite Arab
opposition which at times developed into violence. If the Jews
were to win their homeland, then they would have to lay claim by
greatly increasing the Jewish population (the Arabs were still much
in the majority) and acquiring land and property. During the years
of the British mandate, Britain was clearly uneasy about developments in Palestine, but appeared to be keen not to upset either the
local Arab or the newly settled Jewish communities.

With the onset of the Second World War the persecution of Jews
reached vast and horrifying scales in Nazi Germany and the
pressure for the Jews to have their own homeland became overwhelming. The violence inside Palestine increased as well, not just
with continuing friction between the Arabs and the British, and the
Arabs and the Jews, but also between armed organisations created
by the Jewish community and the British authorities. These organisations were working to force Britain to give up the mandate by
making Palestine ungovernable. By a series of shootings and bomb
attacks (the blowing up of the King David's Hotel in Jerusalem in

July 1946 resulted in heavy British loss of life), the pressure was applied. In the end, the policy was successful.

In April 1947, Britain turned the Palestine problem over to the hands of the United Nations. A plan was drawn up to end the mandate and to partition Palestine into two independent states, with the capital, Jerusalem, being given a special international status. The plan was met with bitter hostility by the Arabs but eventually accepted, after some hesitation, by the Zionists. And a resolution at the United Nations was duly passed: Palestine was to be partitioned. Amid worsening bloodshed, Arabs began leaving. The refugee problem was born.

The Jewish groups in Palestine used the opportunity provided by the last few months of the British mandate to seize as much land as possible, and to terrorise the Arab population as much as they could in the hope that as many as possible would leave. And the fear that they engendered in the Arabs was such that thousands of them did leave. Estimates of the exact figure vary, but it's reckoned that from the time the partition plan was announced towards the close of 1947 and the end of the British mandate in May the following year, between 300 000 and 400 000 Palestinians left their homes and land.

British troops finally left Palestine in May 1948, and the state of Israel was created. Arab armies attacked the new state, but theirs was not an impressive or well co-ordinated fighting force and it made no dent on the newly formed country. On the contrary, Israel had acquired even more territory than had been allocated to it under the original UN partition plan. Furthermore, plans for giving international status to Jerusalem came to nothing. So, the city that is sacred to the three major religions, Judaism, Christianity and Islam, was divided between Jewish West and Arab East. What was left of Arab Palestine, that is to say the area between the eastern boundary of the new state of Israel and the West Bank of the River Jordan was taken over by the Jordanians. The bones of the Middle East conflict and the Palestinian problem as we know them today had been formed.

My first visits to Jerusalem were as a child living in the Jordanian capital, Amman. It was a full day's outing, broken sometimes by a stop at the Dead Sea, the lowest place on earth, or at Jericho where the orange groves provided welcome greenery and shade after the dusty drive from Amman. On one occasion we went to Jerusalem for the opening of a branch of the British bank which my father worked for. The bank is still there today, opposite the Damascus Gate in the tall grey walls of the Old City. But it's shuttered up now; the sign over the door is faded and begrimed with filth. Placards and posters, old and peeling, cover the walls and shutters. The bank, which operates in the Arab world and therefore, by definition, not in Israel, closed down in 1967 after the next Middle East War, when the Israelis took over Arab East Jerusalem and the West Bank. (East Jerusalem was formally annexed to Israel.) The Six Day War of June 1967 was a full Middle East conflict in the sense that it involved the armies of Israel, Egypt, Jordan and Syria. But while the Arab armies were resoundingly defeated, the biggest losers were once again the Palestinian people. An estimated 200 000 of them crossed eastwards over the River Jordan, swelling the refugee population there. For many families, it was their second move. (Until recently you could still see the abandoned refugee camps near Jericho.) For many families too, it was not to be their last forced uprooting.

The Arab world as a whole was shocked and humiliated by the 1967 defeat. For the Palestinians it was the final sign that the Arabs simply did not have the ability or willingness to co-ordinate their policies sufficiently to build an army strong enough to defeat Israel. During the 1950s and '60s they had listened to the oratory of President Nasser and other advocates of pan-Arabism who argued that they first had to work for Arab unity, before they could turn their attention to liberating Palestine. By the mid-60s, though, that oratory was beginning to sound hollow and the 1967 defeat was also the defeat of pan-Arabism. Before this, however, a number of Palestinians had come to the conclusion that if anything was to be done, then they had to do it themselves and not wait for their fellow Arabs to help.

Among the politically active Palestinian students in Cairo in the '50s was Yasir Arafat, the man who was to become the symbol both of the Palestine Liberation Organisation and the whole Palestinian cause. With him at the time were three other men who were later also to be prominent members of the PLO. They met up again in Kuwait in 1959 where Yasir Arafat, after working in the Public Works Ministry, had set up his own contracting business. Here, the first notions of an armed organisation with the declared aim of liberating Palestinian land were discussed. In 1959 Fateh (meaning 'victory') came into being: the letters were also the initials written in reverse of the Arabic for the Palestinian Liberation Movement.

71

The creation of the PLO came five years later, following a decision taken at an Arab summit in Cairo.

Attempts were made to set up a guerrilla network inside the occupied territories. A number of operations were carried out, but they met with tough retaliation from the Israelis. Some guerrillas were killed, many were arrested; dozens of homes of families accused of being associated with the resistance movement were destroyed. A decision was taken to use neighbouring Jordan as a base for raids against the Israelis. By this time Fateh was taking the lead. In the following year (1969) Yasir Arafat became the Chairman of the Palestine Liberation Organisation, and Fateh became the dominant group within the PLO. The pattern for the next decade was set.

The early 1970s saw the start of a series of reverses that the PLO Chairman and his organisation were to suffer over the subsequent sixteen years. And they started in Jordan. For each guerrilla operation brought heavy Israeli retaliation against Jordan, and also the King and his advisers believed that the presence of such a large and hot-headed armed force on his soil could endanger the throne. The final straw was the hijacking of three airliners to an airstrip in Jordan, an act which the Jordanians considered a gross violation of their territory. The King thought long and hard before acting; after all, more than half the population of Jordan is Palestinian. But when his mind was made up he acted decisively and ruthlessly. Led by the King's tough and loyal bedouin troops, the Jordanian army attacked PLO positions and refugee camps in the capital. A few Jordanian troops sided with the Palestinians, but it was no contest. The Palestinians were soundly defeated. The PLO, having suffered its first serious bruising, had no choice but to find a new base. This it found to the north of Israel, in Lebanon.

Born out of that fighting in Jordan in September 1970 was 'Black September', an organisation bent on attacking both Israeli and Jordanian targets wherever they might be found. In the autumn of 1972, members of 'Black September' shocked the world by carrying out an operation at the Olympic Games in Munich. They took eleven Israeli athletes hostage. In the end, after a shoot-out with West German police, all the Israelis and five Palestinians were killed.

Yasir Arafat and his advisers concluded that operations such as that at Munich were counter-productive. And so a move was made to restrain 'Black September'. In the process, however, a new organisation appeared which was to be both a danger and an embarrassment to the PLO in the years to come. It was founded by a man called Sabri al-Banna, better known as Abu Nidal, who split from Fateh in 1974. His underground organisation, operating at different times from Iraq, Syria and Libya, assassinated leading figures in the PLO. Fateh condemned him to death in his absence.

The embarrassment that the Abu Nidal group has caused results from operations that have been blamed on the mainstream of the PLO. In June 1982, for example, the Israeli Ambassador to Britain was shot in London. It was widely accepted that this was the work of the Abu Nidal group; but the Israelis chose to use the shooting as the pretext for carrying out their long-planned invasion of Lebanon to try to wipe out the PLO presence there. And in 1985, just as Yasir Arafat was succeeding in winning international support for a PLO role in Middle East peace negotiations, the Abu Nidal group carried out two bloody attacks on the Israeli airline departure desks at Rome and Vienna airports in which many innocent people were killed. The world did not choose to see the distinction between Abu Nidal and the PLO, and the image of Yasir Arafat and the Palestinians as a whole suffered great international damage.

The period from the early 1970s until 1982 was characterised by the establishment of what amounted to a state within a state in Lebanon. In the absence of a strong central authority, the PLO had a free hand, setting up their own factories, schools and hospitals, in addition to military camps. In many ways it was a period of exuberance for the Palestinians there; many felt they were rehearsing for the day when the 'state' structure would be transferred to Palestine itself. But the period in Lebanon was accompanied by tragedy all the way.

For a start there was the Lebanese civil war which began in 1975. Certain left-wing groups of the PLO became involved in bloody conflict almost as soon as the Muslim–Christian battles began, joining sides with the joint Muslim and nationalist forces. However, by the time the worst of the war was over, Palestinian fighters from all groups had abandoned their positions close to the border with Israel in southern Lebanon to join battle, both with Christian militiamen and, for a time, with the Syrian army. It was during this period that Yasir Arafat and President Assad of Syria developed a mutual loathing which was to last for many years and was to sour relations between Syria and the mainstream of Fateh thereafter.

Throughout the civil war there were appalling acts of butchery committed by all sides; hundreds of Christians were massacred, for example, in the town of Damour, just south of Beirut. And many hundreds of Palestinians died during the siege of a Palestinian refugee camp in East Beirut known as Tel al-Zaatar. The siege, which lasted several months, has entered the folklore of the Palestinian people and is included in poems and songs that lament their fate. The ruins of Tel al-Zaatar (and Damour) are there to this day, bleak and eerie monuments of recent history.

During this period, the PLO used its bases in southern Lebanon to launch raids against Israel and to fire rockets across the border. And as had happened in Jordan, the Israelis hit back hard. In March 1978 there was a particularly brutal attack. A Fateh team landed by sea in Israel and hijacked a bus filled with civilians. In the ensuring shoot-out, nearly forty people were killed. This prompted the Israelis to launch a full-scale invasion of southern Lebanon. Hundreds of Palestinians and Lebanese were killed. It was the determination of the US under President Carter which forced the Israelis to withdraw, and the United Nations Security Council set up an interim force (UNIFIL) to supervise the pull-out. Eight years later the Israelis still had not withdrawn completely, and UNIFIL was still deployed, its mandate never completed.

The UNIFIL units established good relations with local PLO commanders but were continually harassed by the Israelis and their client (mainly Christian) militia which controlled a strip inside Lebanon close to the Israeli border. The international force had neither the weapons nor the mandate to stop the invading Israeli army in June 1982.

At the outset the military operation was given the misleading title 'Operation Peace for Galilee', the stated intention being to launch a quick attack to remove those positions which had been firing rockets on settlements in Galilee. In reality, though, there had been no such attacks for a year following an unofficial ceasefire arranged through the good offices of the United Nations, with American help.

Very soon, as the army swept north backed by air power and facing a guerrilla organisation ill-equipped to fight a conventional war, it became clear that the intention of the Israelis was something much grander. Palestinian camps in Tyre and Sidon were flattened; and PLO fighters were forced to retreat further and further, until they were bottled up in the western half of Beirut.

I returned to Lebanon at this time, docking at Jounieh and driving down to East Beirut. I remember being shocked at the sight of Israeli soldiers relaxing and driving around an Arab city. From East Beirut, a young Sunni Muslim driver agreed to take me across the notoriously dangerous 'Green Line' which emerged in the civil war and separates the Christian east of the city from the predominantly Muslim west. As we set out, an air raid was starting, so we turned back to wait for it to finish. Then, off again. 'How do we get past the Israeli blockade?' I asked. 'Easy,' the driver said, smiling and pointing to a plastic carrier bag at his feet. It contained bread and fruit, both apparently much in demand from the Israeli troops. Indeed, throughout the siege, foreign reporters were always able to get in and out of West Beirut. In the last resort, American dollars softened the hearts of the toughest Israelis.

This was no comfort, though, for the Lebanese caught up in the horrifying bombardment that seemed to go on day and night, from land, sea and sky for days over a period of weeks. The sights and sounds of this time, the thunder of gun-boats opening up from just off the coast, the whine of the dive-bombers and the crunch that shook the inside of your body as the bombs landed – they have stuck in my mind like a permanent nightmare. The Israelis cut off the water supply, food was scarce, there was no electricity, and the rubbish piled up in the streets. Probably we will never know how many people died in that siege. Certainly the impression at the time was that the majority of casualties were civilians. For while Palestinian areas of the city came under blanket bombardment, the PLO fighters had set up a warren of underground shelters which gave them protection most ordinary people did not have. In the end, Yasir Arafat said the city and its civilian population should suffer no more, and he agreed to move his fighters out, under the supervision of the Red Cross, and American and French troops. The sixty-seven day siege has become known as the 'Battle of Beirut' and is another event that has found its way into Palestinian nationalist poems and songs.

So too has another tragedy that was soon to follow. Once the evacuation was complete, the Americans pulled out, despite a promise which the PLO says they made to protect Palestinian civilians left behind in the camps. On 14 September 1982, the newly elected President of Lebanon, Bashir Gemayel, was assassinated. The Israelis then moved into West Beirut and took up positions near the Sabra and Chatila Palestinian refugee camps. For two days they stood by as Christian militiamen went in to 'mop up the resistance' there. The carnage was on a scale that reporters who eventually were allowed into the camps found hard to describe. Certainly many hundreds, some people say as many as 3000 people (men, women and children) were massacred. After the ensuing international outcry, the Americans put together another multi-national force to go into Beirut.

Just over a year later, many of those PLO fighters who had climbed aboard the ships in Beirut harbour were being evacuated once more from Lebanon. With their few belongings crammed into carrier bags and battered suitcases and carrying their automatic rifles they were ferried in lorries down to the port of Tripoli in the north of the country. A rebellion had broken out within Fateh over Yasir Arafat's leadership. The PLO Chairman had been ordered out of Syria, and the Syrians had been backing an assault led by PLO dissidents against the Arafat forces cornered in Tripoli, having been routed from their positions in the Bekaa valley. At dawn every morning in December 1983 it was our unpleasant and very frightening task to drive into Tripoli to report on how the battle was progressing. Long before we reached the first Syrian army checkpoints on the approaches to Tripoli we could see the pale dawn sky blackened by a huge pall of smoke which belched for weeks out of the burning oil refinery in the city. The procedure was to stop at a hotel on a ridge just outside Tripoli, listen to how intense the fighting seemed and then decide whether or not to go in. Once the decision was taken, it was a matter of driving flat out through the chicane of earth barricades, through the debris-covered streets to the part of the town where the PLO had their offices. Tours of the hospitals revealed dozens of appalling injuries to fighters and civilians alike. Outside one hospital a deep-freeze container lorry was packed with corpses, the mortuary, like the wards, being full to overflowing. The Palestinian Red Crescent Society had been forced by the fighting to abandon their hospitals in the nearby refugee camps and had set up a makeshift clinic in the cramped and dark basement of a school. Hundreds of miles from occupied Palestinian land, here were Palestinians fighting one another. It all seemed particularly sad and pointless.

During the fighting in Tripoli there were many predictions that this was the end of Yasir Arafat. But once again he bounced back; indeed, among what is arguably the most important Palestinian constituency, that living on the West Bank and Gaza Strip, the siege of Tripoli greatly enhanced Mr Arafat's prestige. For in their view, he had stood and fought for Palestinian independence in the face of PLO men who had 'sold out' to Syria.

Yasir Arafat, while small in stature, is one of the giants of the Arab world. His fellow Arabs either love or hate him with a passion that is reserved for only a handful of leaders. He is, whether one loves him or hates him, a remarkable man, possibly the biggest asset that the Palestinian people at large have had. His picture, with his unshaven face and the black-and-white *kaffiyeh* on his head, is recognised around the world, and every time his face appears in a newspaper or on a television screen the world is reminded of that cause. Among the majority of Palestinian people, and especially among those living under Israeli occupation, 'Abu Ammar' (his *nom-de-guerre*, by which he is most widely known in the Arab world) is not only the most popular leader, but also the living hope that one day they will be free of occupation. As one of his former aides said: 'He is the Palestinian tragedy incarnate. He's always on the move, but still an outcast in the eyes of most Arab leaders.'

Always on the move. There is no leader in the world who travels as much as Yasir Arafat. He flits from capital to capital in a private jet, never announcing his exact programme for fear of an attempt on his life, and maintaining a punishing daily schedule which even the toughest young followers find impossible to keep up with. 'It's not physically possible,' a former aide told me 'to accompany him for a full year.' Mr Arafat is unmarried ('He's married to the Palestinian cause,' the former aide said) and is a tireless worker, managing on very little sleep. His colleagues say too that he is exasperatingly stubborn and will argue endlessly to get his way in discussions. To meet he can be exceptionally charming; on a public platform he is a master, winning over his audience with a mixture of powerful oratory, humour and theatre. At the meeting of the Palestinian parliament in exile in Jordan in 1984, Mr Arafat was seated at the front of the auditorium, not on the stage. But he might just as well have been. He took a passionate interest in every detail of the agenda, leaping up from his seat and gesticulating to the chair whenever he had a point to make, waving his arms as though he were conducting an orchestra. And towards the end of the meetings when his policies came in for criticism, with the timing of a professional actor he announced, with a tremble in his voice, that he would be resigning as leader. The gesture had the desired effect: he was carried shoulder high back onto the podium.

Financing for the PLO comes in large measure from the oil-producing states in the Gulf, foremost of which is Saudi Arabia. Much of Yasir Arafat's job as roving ambassador is to seek funds. Nearly everywhere he goes he is received like a president, and his critics say he behaves too much like one. He has been accused of keeping personal charge of PLO funds, of being too autocratic and of having a flamboyant life-style incompatible with that of a guerrilla leader. Mr Arafat has always had the difficult task of balancing his twin roles of statesman and fighter, as well as balancing the various factions within the PLO with their differing views on what the organisation's policy should be. He has not always been successful. Since 1983 the PLO has been split between those groups which accept Mr Arafat's leadership and those based in Syria, who reject it.

In the end, the battle that Mr Arafat has had to fight within the region has been one to keep his organisation independent of any particular Arab regime and also to try to encourage those regimes to do more to help the Palestinian cause. For in a number of Arab countries there is little love lost between the Palestinians and the local population. And at times of crises, as we have seen, the Arabs have done little to help. For example, during the Israeli invasion of Lebanon in 1982, the Syrian armed forces did battle for a short time, but no other army came to the aid of the PLO. And Mr Arafat was deeply angered by the comment by Colonel Qadafi of Libya at the time of the evacuation from Beirut. He said the PLO fighters should remain put and die.

On the political level, it was agreed at an Arab summit in Rabat in Morocco in 1974 that the PLO was the 'sole legitimate representative of the Palestine people.' However, as the PLO became more fragmented, and as its leadership vacillated, so the Palestinians living under harsh Israeli occupation watched their land disappear by the day as new 'settlements' (they are actually high-rise townships, fortress-like in looks) and new roads scarred the landscape. On a recent visit to the West Bank I stood looking across one valley which has not yet been spoilt to where the ancient Monastery of St George lies far away nestled into the rocks. The moment of tranquil thought lasted only a few seconds, soon shattered by low-flying Israeli jets on exercise. It seemed to sum up a lot.

The longer too that a solution to the Palestinian problem remains elusive, the more embittered will become the thousands of refugees living in camps in Jordan and Lebanon. Among the generation born and brought up in the camps, as well as among the same group living under Israeli occupations, there is a sense of anger and frustration that is beginning to spill over more and more often into violence. It's a trend that older generations are viewing with alarm. To recognise this trend does not excuse the acts of terror carried out by Palestinians, but it goes some way towards explaining it.

For one has to understand that conditions in the refugee camps are appalling. There are no streets as such, just alleys of baked mud. A drain runs down the middle of them, which is totally inadequate when it rains. The alleyways thread their way through a maze of squalid breeze-block buildings, inadequate for keeping out the rain and cold. When news reaches these camps of an act of terror carried out somewhere in the world, many people living in the camps will not condemn it. For in the minds of many of the younger generation, the more temperate policies of Mr Arafat and his supporters have been discredited. Negotiations have not brought back Palestine. For them, violence is the only option left.

It's a trend, of course, that worries Palestinian leaders too. For the more the younger generation take matters into their own hands, the more difficult it will be for the Palestinians as a whole to convince the world that they are a community prepared to live in peace, albeit under certain conditions. These leaders also need the refugees living in camps to keep alive the notion that they are only temporary bases and that one day they will be able to return to their homelands.

With every day that passes too, Israel's hold on the occupied territories gets stronger. There are so many new townships, so many Israeli troops around that it's easy to forget that it is in fact land under occupation. And there is certainly no significant body of Israelis who are prepared to consider giving up even part of the occupied territories. Furthermore, all Israelis agree that East Jerusalem, site of the Wailing Wall and the third most sacred shrine in Islam, the Al-Aqsa mosque, will never be surrendered.

Because the Palestinian issue hits the headlines most frequently when the PLO says or does something, there's a danger of equating the organisation with the whole body of Palestinians around the world. Many leading Palestinians are critical of the PLO, many ordinary people do not approve of it or the way it operates. But virtually all of them deplore the split because it is the only body in the world that represents them and it is unlikely that any alternative can emerge. The Palestinians as a group are among the brightest and the most professionally successful in the Arab world. They hold many top managerial and academic jobs not just in Jordan but in several other Arab countries. It could be argued that they deserve a better leadership – one that could have been more flexible and less cumbersome. I believe there is a danger that the current leadership may be judged by historians as having been one that missed too many chances in the search for peace and was too slow to learn the necessity of winning world public opinion and keeping it on its side.

By the end of 1986 the future of the PLO was as unclear as ever. In February of that year King Hussein of Jordan announced that efforts to work out a joint approach with Mr Arafat in the search for a Middle East peace settlement had failed. In the end Mr Arafat refused to recognise the United Nations Resolution 242 which, among other things, implicitly recognises Israel's right to exist. In the subsequent months many of the PLO offices in Amman were shut down and the PLO presence as a whole scaled down almost to nothing. Once again Mr Arafat was without a base in any of the countries bordering Israel. At the same time, relations with the authorities in Tunis, where the PLO headquarters were established in 1983, were becoming strained.

Furthermore there was evidence, as King Hussein looked for an alternative Palestinian leadership which might join Jordan in the peace process, that the PLO had not abandoned the armed struggle within the occupied territories. The PLO office in Cairo was quick to admit responsibility in October 1986 for a grenade attack against a group of Israeli soldiers near the Wailing Wall in Jerusalem.

For the Palestinian people, links with their homeland are maintained through the arts: songs, plays and literature, steeped in nationalist sentiments, form the basis of the recent cultural heritage. But crafts too, such as pottery, with its bold swirling blue patterns, and weaving and embroidery, continue wherever Palestinians are to be found. Such activities help keep up morale. For the fact is that for Palestinians living in the squalor of the refugee camps, an independent Palestine still seems a very, very long way away.

6 Jordan and Syria

A kingdom looking West, a republic looking East

Jordan

The taxi steered its way through the heavy traffic of central Amman and headed up one of the hills on and around which the city is built. On the left we passed the railway station, a stop on the famous Hejaz railway line that ran from Damascus through to what is now Saudi Arabia, a line which was made famous because of the acts of sabotage carried out on it by Lawrence of Arabia. The sight of the station revived the skeleton of a memory of being a child of about four. We were heading up this hill on the way to the airport with a picnic in the boot of the car; we were on our way to watch my father play cricket.

Amman's civilian airport has now been relocated inconveniently to a position some 20 miles south of the capital. It was chosen and named – as was the national airline – in memory of Queen Alia who died in a helicopter crash at that spot in the desert. The old airport is now used only for military and VIP flights. And it was in order to be present when King Hussein met a visiting British dignitary that I was travelling up this particular hill once more. As I watched King Hussein walk the length of the red carpet past the smartly dressed and crisply drilled guard of honour to greet his guest I could remember those games of cricket on Fridays thirty years ago, this English peculiarity being contested on a concrete wicket covered by matting on the desert between the apron and the runway. And on more than one occasion as we watched from the boundary rope an RAF Hawker Hunter jet was practising landings and take-offs in the background. The pilot was King Hussein.

Thirty years on, even after frequent visits to Jordan in recent times, I still experience the thrill of discovering fresh echoes of my earliest memories. And through all the years when so many of the early childhood memories have faded, King Hussein has stayed in power and has continued to fly aeroplanes, defying political pressures and the assassins' bullets. For the modern story of Jordan is the story of the survival of King Hussein and his country in the face of what at times have seemed overwhelming odds.

Jordan is one of the Arab countries born out of the machinations of Britain and France as they carved up the Middle East among themselves at the end of the First World War, and her boundaries reflect more the whims of the colonial officials who drew lines on the map with their rulers and pencils than any natural land frontiers. During the First World War the Ottoman Turks, whose empire spread down the east Mediterranean coast into the Hejaz, sided with Germany. Britain therefore decided to encourage the Arabs to revolt against the Ottomans. The revolt was spearheaded by the Sharif Hussein of Mecca, the head of the Hashemite clan which had been dominant in the Holy City since the eleventh century. His son, Amir Faisal, was the military commander and Faisal's main (though by no means only) British card was Lawrence of Arabia, whose role was to direct military operations. In return for this revolt, the Arabs were promised British support for an independent Arab state. Behind the backs of the Arabs, though, Britain and France had worked out a plan (the Sykes–Picot agreement of 1916) to divide the area between their two spheres of influence. The result of this betrayal was that while Amir Faisal had assumed power in Damascus, he was soon ousted by the French, only to be whisked onto the throne (with or without the wishes of the people) in the Iraqi capital, Baghdad, to guarantee that British interests there were safeguarded. His brother, Abdullah, in the meantime, marched in from the Hejaz with the aim of avenging his brother. This he never did, but he did succeed in taking over much of the territory which is now known as Jordan today. The British, from 1923 onwards – perhaps in an attempt to appease their guilt at their broken promise to the Hashemites – encouraged the Amir Abdullah to develop the state of Transjordan, albeit with a strong contingent of British political and military advisers. In 1946, Transjordan became independent, with Abdullah being proclaimed king, but still with a strong British grip on the wheel.

The creation of the state of Israel gave King Abdullah the chance to annex the territories to the west of the River Jordan up to and including the eastern half of Jerusalem (the area now known as the West Bank). The King was keen on the idea of Greater Syria, which in his mind would encompass the Arab countries of the eastern Mediterranean along with Iraq. Arab nationalists, especially those in Egypt, smelt a rat. They believed King Abdullah, in pursuit of his own dreams of grandeur, might do a deal with Israel, accepting the borders as they stood after the war following that country's independence. In any event, Transjordan, a country of mostly bedouin stock, joined forces with a largely reluctant but beaten and dispirited population of Palestinians to form the modern state of Jordan. But the birth was soon marked by violence. Perhaps because of outside Arab fears of what he might be scheming, the King was assassinated in July 1951 at the Al-Aqsa mosque in Jerusalem. His son Talal succeeded him, but not for long. Because of mental instability he had no choice but to make way for his own son Hussein, a youth of seventeen who had been with his grandfather when he was assassinated. In 1952 King Hussein stepped onto the world stage. He has been there ever since.

The early 1950s, where in my mind I can detect the first etchings of memory, was a period when Arab nationalism as an ideal flourished. For the young King, this must have been a lonely and difficult period. In one ear he took the counsel of the British, in the other he was hearing the denunciations of the radicals; and all the time he lacked the backing of the biggest kingdom in the region, Saudi Arabia, because of traditional clan rivalries – the Saud family having driven the remaining Hashemites out of Mecca and the Hejaz. The backbone of the King's military strength lay with the Arab Legion, a force of bedouin soldiers led by British officers which had been formed some thirty years earlier. They were well trained and disciplined, fiercely loyal to the King, and highly effective. In the 1950s the force was led by the late Sir John Glubb, known universally as Glubb Pasha.

Glubb the soldier is how he will be remembered. 'He was a very good professional soldier', General Sir John Hackett wrote in an obituary. 'He was without any doubt a better handler of Bedu than Lawrence (of Arabia) ever was.' My memory, though, is of a friendly but chaotic family home in Amman, full of noise, children and animals – domestic and wild. I remember a Siamese cat called Anna and small exotic birds, and there were certainly some dogs; and on one occasion I remember seeing a gazelle quietly chewing at the arm of a sofa in the living room, something that appeared to be of no concern to the family.

Glubb Pasha was greatly admired by his men. As late as 1985 a very senior officer in the Jordanian army spoke with genuine affection of his days serving under the Pasha and said he made a point of seeing him whenever he was in Britain. But in the mid-1950s, with the tide of Arab nationalism gathering strength, a British officer commanding an Arab fighting force was beginning to look incongruous, particularly in the eyes of those advocating the nationalist cause most ardently.

Matters had started to come to a head in 1955 following the formation of the Baghdad Pact, an anti-communist grouping which linked Iraq, Turkey, Iran and Pakistan, and of which Britain was a member. Jordan came under British pressure to join too but the Baghdad Pact flew straight into the face of Arab nationalism, and this was exactly the sort of imperialist interference in the affairs of the region that the nationalists wanted to be rid of. President Nasser of Egypt, through the 'Voice of the Arabs' radio station in Cairo, beamed his rejection of the pact into every home in the region which possessed a radio. Rioting broke out in Amman. I was kept out of sight in the house. I remember little else now (it was January 1956), except being frightened by the sound of a mob shouting angrily, and my mother urging my father to ring Glubb Pasha for help as part of the crowd surged through our garden. Other snippets of memory survive too: my father, despite the fear and tension in our house, insisting on listening to a football commentary on the radio (his team, Bristol Rovers, were playing Manchester United); my mother and I being driven in an Arab Legion car through a wrecked but deserted city centre the next morning before the curfew was enforced; and a long and anxious wait at the airport for a plane to take us out of Amman, uncertain all the while what was happening to my father.

A few months after the riots, in March 1956 King Hussein won broad popular acclaim in Jordan and elsewhere in the Arab world by summarily dismissing Glubb Pasha from his post and giving the man who'd dedicated his life to the country a few hours to leave. It was the end of a chapter in Middle East history.

The subsequent months saw Jordan moving closer to the nationalist side of the fence; relations with neighbouring states improved considerably. But the King has always been clever enough not to align himself too strongly with any trend in the region. And indeed in 1957 when he judged that the pendulum had swung too far he stepped in, dissolving parliament and political parties, and in no uncertain terms pushed the pendulum back, reinforcing Jordan's economic and political links with the West in general, but with the United States – the main aid donor – in particular.

This was a move which served only to make Jordan look even more isolated from the prevailing currents in the region, and not for the first or last time there were predictions that the monarchy could not survive – predictions that that seemed more like certainties when the Hashemite monarchy in Baghdad was hacked down in July 1958. But King Hussein survived, gradually developing industries and building up the economy (with Palestinians very often taking the initiative) and gradually encouraging tourism. Jordan could offer not just the Christian and Muslim sacred sites in the Old City of Jerusalem but also the Roman city of Jerash and Petra, the Nabatean city hewn out of the rock which glows pink in the dawn light and in my opinion rates as one of the wonders of the world.

If the Arab republics with one voice denounced Jordan as being a tool of Western imperialism, those countries were continuing to argue among themselves as ideologies clashed and as flimsy structures of inter-state unions collapsed almost before they were completed.

All the time, though, the King was having to keep an eye on his western neighbour and enemy, Israel, and on the Palestinian community within his own borders, some of them living in refugee camps, some of them successful businessmen, but all of them bitter that their country had been snatched from them. Not without considerable misgivings did King Hussein agree with other Arab heads of state on the idea of creating the Palestine Liberation Organisation (PLO) and it was equally with some reluctance that Jordan took part in the Six Day War with Israel in June 1967. The war was a disaster for the whole Arab world, but no country suffered the direct effect of it more than Jordan, because Israel captured Jordanian territory – East Jerusalem and the West Bank. Aside from military and material losses, some 200 000 Palestinian refugees crossed over the River Jordan onto the East Bank.

And as the newly formed PLO started to try to avenge the defeat of the war by carrying out guerrilla attacks against Israeli targets from bases within Jordan, the Jordanians had to suffer heavy Israeli retaliation. The PLO military and political presence in Jordan, meanwhile, had swollen to such an extent that the monarchy itself seemed to be under threat from within. As East Bank Jordanians began to resent more and more the freedom that the PLO accorded itself within their country, clashes broke out between the guerrillas and the Jordanian army. Matters came to a head in September 1970 when the King ordered his troops to drive the PLO forces out of Jordan. After heavy fighting in Amman and in the camps just outside, the PLO fighters were defeated (see

Chapter 5) leaving a pool of bitterness and suspicion separating King Hussein and the PLO Chairman, Mr Yasir Arafat, which, despite public acts of reconciliation, has never been completely removed.

King Hussein was saddened bitterly by the loss of East Jerusalem containing the Al-Aqsa mosque and the Dome of the Rock – among the most sacred places in Islam. And as a member of the Hashemite family from Mecca he has always felt it his duty to recover East Jerusalem for the Arabs. The King concluded, furthermore, after the defeat of 1967, that the Arabs would not be able to regain it by force. So Jordan stayed out of the October 1973 war with Israel as much as possible, doing its utmost not to provoke an Israeli assault across the River Jordan, but at the same time sending troops to fight alongside the Syrians.

Partly because of this sense of responsibility, King Hussein always felt that he and his country were best placed to represent the interests of the Palestinian people. However, with the PLO growing in military and political strength, this assumption was up for challenge. In the end, King Hussein had no choice but to accept a decision taken by Arab heads of state meeting in Rabat in Morocco in 1974. This declared that the PLO was 'the sole legitimate representative of the Palestinian people'. Despite the King's exasperation and anger about the PLO on many occasions in the years that followed, he has always said that he will abide by the Rabat decision.

In the subsequent years, the King has been doing his best to promote efforts to achieve peace in the region. He has good practical reasons for wanting to do this apart from any idealistic ones. For a start the majority of people in Jordan are Palestinians who are becoming increasingly frustrated at the failure of all peace efforts so far. In recent months the numbers have been growing as thousands of Palestinians who had been working in the Gulf States have been laid off by the recession there and have had nowhere else to go. The King recognises that a disaffected Palestinian community could cause trouble, either by provoking an Israeli backlash against Jordan, or else, at a time of economic problems and growing unemployment, by threatening the monarchy through social unrest. The King has said on numerous occasions that time is running out if there is to be a solution of the Palestinian problem. What he means is that every day sees more Arab land on the West Bank being acquired by the Israelis. And he fears that right-wing

Israelis will carry out their threat to force the creation of a Palestinian state in Jordan.

The failure of the United States to support him sufficiently in his search for a Middle East settlement, combined with Washington's apparently blind support for Israel, has led King Hussein to become disillusioned and depressed about the country which he wanted to consider his best friend and ally. Often, even when Washington has deemed it right to help Jordan by, for example, selling weapons, Congress has blocked the deal, forcing Jordan to turn to the Soviet Union instead. In an interview early in 1986 King Hussein said the United States had broken off a thirty-year-old military link with Jordan by going back on a promise to supply arms worth more than a billion pounds. The King made no attempt to hide his bitterness. 'In terms of our needs and requirements, the United States has stopped being the major supplier of defensive weapons to Jordan,' he said. And he went on to say that the latest about-turn in Washington had undermined the credibility of the US government in terms of promises and commitments. Referring to his belief that Israel might try to destabilise Jordan he said he was no longer confident that Washington would restrain the Israelis. 'In the past,' the King continued, 'I used to take seriously assurances from our friends.' But in the light of recent events and the growing influence of Jewish organisations on US policy he could no longer be sure.

The King is bitter too about the attitude of the PLO and its leader Mr Yasir Arafat. He believes that the PLO has been neither sufficiently flexible nor sufficiently courageous to take the risks needed if a peace settlement were to be achieved.

Matters came to a head in February 1986. Exactly a year earlier the King and Mr Arafat had agreed to work jointly to try to find a solution to the Middle East problem that would give self-determination to the Palestinian people. This would come through negotiations at an international conference attended by all the parties to the conflict and the five permanent members of the Security Council of the United Nations. (This is the formula advocated by most Arab countries, although it does not enjoy the support of Israel or the United States which both oppose Soviet participation in the peace process.)

But after lengthy negotiations and much vacillation on the part of Mr Arafat, the PLO Chairman in the end could not make the last political step needed. He refused to accept UN Resolution 242 which, among other things, recognises Israel's right to exist. Such a step, the King said, in a lengthy and angry speech in February 1986, would have paved the way to talks with the United States. He accused Mr Arafat of going back on his word and said he was unable to work with PLO leaders 'until such time as their word becomes their bond characterised by commitment, credibility and constancy.' In the months that followed, PLO offices in Jordan were shut down and Mr Arafat's deputy and military commander Abu Jihad ordered out of the country.

Since then King Hussein has announced plans to inject millions of dollars of aid into the occupied territories. In part this is to improve the living and working conditions of Palestinians there and to stem the flow of Palestinians into Jordan for the King is aware that some right-wing politicians in Israel believe that the inhabitants of the West Bank should be forced to move to Jordan and that Jordan should become Palestine. The aid is also designed to win support for Jordan among West Bankers, the majority of whom have been traditional supporters of Yasir Arafat.

Also of concern to Jordan these days is the progress of the Gulf War. King Hussein has been a loyal supporter of Iraq since the start of the conflict. Jordan has allowed the Iraqis to use the port of Aqaba to give the Iraqis access to the sea, and Jordanian officers are frequent visitors to the battle front. His support is not prompted by the fear that there would be a rise of fundamentalism within its own borders if the Iranians should defeat Iraq; rather the fear is of the effects of the political and economic disruption which would hit the whole region in the event of an Iranian victory, leaving the chances of a Middle East peace settlement looking bleaker than ever.

All these strains and disappointments have made King Hussein a tired man. At a briefing in his palace a few months ago, with the photographs and ornaments presented by visiting heads of state and other dignitaries placed in the room all around him, he seemed to have aged visibly. Smoking a cigarette, his voice was at times almost inaudible with strain as he spoke again about the failure of American policy and the failure of the USA to deliver promised terms. 'This is not the way,' the King said, 'to deal with problems among friends.' That day, I sensed, the King felt he had few friends.

The King's palace, sandstone in colour and with a cluster of aerials on the roof reflecting his hobby as a radio ham, stands in grounds which are rich with trees, shrubs and flowers on one of the hills close to the centre of the city. A large garage, with the doors open, reveals a collection of vehicles, again reflecting an interest of the King. Some of the vehicles are for children, of which he has four by his current wife, Queen Noor. She is an American and is the King's fourth wife. Even royal weddings bring back personal memories; in 1955 I was left at home to watch, rather frightened I remember, as fireworks streaked across the night sky of Amman to celebrate the King's first marriage, to Princess Dina. My parents had gone to separate wedding parties at the palace, and the famous Egyptian singer Umm Qulthoum had been flown over from Cairo to perform for the occasion.

Other nights I was left at home when my parents went to attend a play or concert in the romantic setting of the amphitheatre in the Roman ruins at Jerash to the north of Amman, ruins which are remarkably well preserved and where you can still see the grooves made by the chariot wheels down some of the streets. Sitting under the stars watching a performance of ballet at a recent Jerash festival on those same stone steps where my parents had sat I felt a sense of continuous history, a tangible link between me, my parents and Jordan with all its store of evocative sounds and sights, like the pink glow that covers the flat-roofed stone houses of Amman at sunset or the watery pale light at dawn – all of which keep childhood memories alive.

Syria

A few months after being forced out of Amman by the riots at the start of 1956 my mother and I were flying out to join my father in his new posting to Aleppo in Syria. What was planned as a two-year stay in that country was cut short after two weeks because of more riots, with the anger this time directed squarely on Britain. The reason: the Suez crisis (see Chapter 3). I have only dim recollections of that period, the most clear being of the shouting crowds which seemed to fill the whole street passing by the apartment building where we lived. On the advice of the British Consul we flew to Beirut but my father stayed. Back in Britain we heard nothing from him for two weeks. The first word we received was that he was in Turkey – he'd made it safely over the border. Working in a British bank had become impossible because of the street anger.

It was not a particularly sweet opening to my association with

Syria. But that display of anti-British feeling, while it was sparked off by events in another country, is indicative of feelings in a country which believes it has suffered as much as, and possibly even more than, others in the region at the hands of foreigners. Since early history the area – on the main east–west trade route and blessed with fertile soil – has been fought over by outsiders. One of the most impressive Crusader castles, the Krak des Chevaliers, on a hill-top between Homs and Tartous, is a reminder of one such incursion. Later the Turks came. I have a map on the wall dated 1838 which shows Syria stretching from Aleppo to the north down to the Dead Sea in the south-east and the Sinai desert in the south-west – a vast swathe of territory divided into *Pashaliks*. As we've seen, the Arab Revolt orchestrated by Britain to oust the Turks failed to produce the promised independence. As the British and the French divided the spoils, France was given authority over both Lebanon and Syria, with the port city of Tripoli being sliced out of Syria and added to Lebanon. To this day the atmosphere in Tripoli is different from that in any other Lebanese city, with many of the people still instinctively looking to Damascus as their capital rather than Beirut.

Syria today, with a population of ten or eleven million, is one of the most powerful and important countries in the region. (I think it is correct to call it, as many people do, the second regional super-power, the other being Israel.) At the same time it is the most mis-understood country and one of the most difficult to penetrate at any level. Reporting of events inside such an immensely important country is minimal because the Syrian authorities do not welcome foreign reporters, fearing adverse publicity and believing that there is a Western conspiracy to denigrate their country. The prob-lem is that this attitude feeds on itself. Once in Syria, information of any kind is hard to acquire. The Syrian people are not used to the free flow of information and are fearful of the Mukhabarat, the secret police, some of whom one can see armed and in plain clothes at all major road junctions in the capital, Damascus. And this general lack of official co-operation tends to leave visiting jour-nalists with little choice but to write what the Syrians complain are 'negative' articles. This is a tragedy, because it has meant that Syria's importance was until recently overlooked, especially in the United States.

The rather inhibited atmosphere can probably be traced back into the country's stormy history, to the years immediately after gaining independence from the French in 1946 when one military coup followed another. It's little wonder that Syria was dismissed in the West as yet another unstable newly independent third-world state. In fact, power changed hands more than a dozen times between independence and the coup that brought the current president, Hafez al-Assad, to power in 1970.

Syria in this period saw the birth of a new ideology in the Middle East with the creation of the Baath Party (*baath* in Arabic means 'renaissance'). It was founded in Damascus in 1944 by a Christian, Michel Aflaq, advocating Arab nationalism and union among Arab countries, and after the departure of the French it emerged in 1946 as a legal political movement. Over the years, with the successive changes of regime, a split appeared in the party and while the Baath is still the ruling group in Syria today, Mr Aflaq and some of his colleagues have been officially discredited and are living in Iraq where a rival branch of the Baath party is in power, one bitterly hostile to Syria.

The Baathists have not been in power exclusively since independence. For three years, beginning in 1958, Syria merged with Egypt under President Nasser under the name of the United Arab Republic. However, like all such attempts in the Arab world, the merger looked better on paper than it did in practice. In 1963 the Baath were back in the driving seat and Syria was once again a separate state.

The military coups in the 1950s and '60s brought to the fore a number of officers from minority religious groups in Syria (the majority of Syrians are Sunni Muslims), especially Druze and Alawites who had traditionally found jobs in the army. The Alawites are an obscure offshoot of the Shiite Islamic faith and account for only a small proportion of the population (one estimate is twelve per cent). A bloody coup in 1966 saw the Alawites occupying the seat of power, where they've been ever since. The die for the Syria we know today was cast in November 1970 when a former fighter pilot who had become minister of defence, General Hafez al-Assad, took over power in a bloodless coup.

President Assad has carved a niche for himself in Middle Eastern history in his own lifetime, being among the handful of truly effective Arab leaders. He lacks the charisma of President Nasser, but he has managed to stay in power longer than most of his colleagues in the region, and much as he is hated in certain parts of the world, he has won the respect of many world leaders as a tough, uncompromising leader who has brought stability to Syria – something that had been elusive since independence. The former American Secretary of State, Henry Kissinger, called him the most interesting man in the Middle East; a former Under Secretary of State, Mr Joseph Sisco, called him 'intelligent, engaging, soft-spoken. He is also Byzantine and has very little compunction about the ruthless use of force. He is a very tough bargainer and his first concern is survival.'

Survival has not always been easy; for the Alawites have not always been popular among certain sections of the Sunni population, holding as they do many of the top jobs within the armed forces and the civilian administration. The main opposition has come from the Sunni fundamentalist group known as the Muslim Brotherhood which in the late 1970s was responsible for the killing of dozens of Alawites and for an attempt on the life of the President himself. In 1980, membership of the Brotherhood was made an offence carrying the death penalty. In 1982 there was a full-scale uprising in the staunchly Sunni Muslim town of Hama which was put down with a massive display of force on the part of the Damascus government – whole areas of the city were razed to the ground, and hundreds of people killed. Since then, the threat from the Muslim Brotherhood has subsided.

On the whole President Assad's attitude to other sects and religions seems to be that they are free to practise how they like (Muslim shops in Damascus close on Fridays, Jewish shops on Saturdays and Christian shops on Sundays). However, he will not tolerate extremists at any price. Generally the Syrians seem happy with this attitude, though it means that Christians and Jews, while they can worship openly and do business like anyone else, have no chance of getting top government jobs. As one Christian in Damascus said to me: 'Sometimes I feel like asking why I can't become president, just because I am a Christian.'

On one of the dusty hills overlooking Damascus, a huge crane sits over a partially completed palace for President Assad. It's been under construction for years; nobody knows when it will be finished. This is appropriate. For in just about everything, President Assad likes to keep people guessing. And just as his portrait adorns almost every corner of the capital, so his influence is all-pervasive. With the confidence that he has the backing of the Alawite community and the armed forces, President Assad is prepared to be stubborn and patient as he works out his plans both for his own country and the region as a whole. The first priority is keeping the Alawites in power. 'The history of Syria being what it is,' one diplomat in Damascus told me, 'there's a big chance of vengeance being wrought on the Alawites if they let things slip out of their hand.'

A major question, indeed, is who will succeed the President. When he was seriously ill in 1983, his brother Rifaat – with a private army of his own and a fortune said to have been made from smuggling goods into Syria – moved against other contenders for power. The president was furious; he rose from his sick-bed and ordered his brother's tanks off the streets of the capital. Rifaat went into what was apparently exile for six months; but he returned and was later made one of three vice-presidents. Whether he is in or out of favour is a continual talking point in Damascus, as is the question of whom Hafez al-Assad has in mind to succeed him. Once again, he likes to keep people guessing.

Much of President Assad's energies are taken up with foreign matters, and at the top of the list is the Arab–Israeli dispute. Syria sees itself as the leading 'confrontation' state and rejects totally the idea of a negotiated peace settlement with Israel on the part of any Arab state until such time as the Arabs can negotiate from a position of equal military strength. Consequently, a third of the budget each year goes on buying weapons and keeping 350 000 men in uniform. President Assad's venom is directed first and foremost at Egypt because of the peace treaty which President Sadat signed with the Israelis, but he lashes out at anyone who seems to be contemplating a deal with the enemy. When in 1985 King Hussein and the PLO Chairman, Mr Yasir Arafat, signed an agreement to try to work out a joint approach to peace negotiations, President Assad let fly: 'Those who want to join Camp David, let them go to hell and get burned alone.'

President Assad is realistic enough to know, though, that there is a long way to go before military parity can be achieved. Syria has received more than one bloody nose at the hands of Israel. In the Arab defeat of 1967, Syria lost the Golan Heights, which were later annexed by Israel. There were severe losses in the 1973 war too. The official media in Damascus made great play of the fact that when Israel invaded Lebanon in 1982 Syria was the only country to fight the invading army. I was in Damascus at the time; one day a captured Israeli tank was driven through the city with the body of a dead Israeli soldier draped across the front. Syrian soldiers, cheering and waving to the crowds, were packed on top of the tank. It was not much of a victory celebration – it came a few hours after Syria had signed a ceasefire which ended its brief and symbolic resistance against the Israeli advance – and was about the only spoil of war that could be mustered. For in reality the Israelis had wiped out Syria's Russian-supplied air-defence system. Syria had no choice but to pull out of the fray.

The Soviet Union has supplied all Syria's arms and military equipment, much of it being the most modern available for Damascus is Moscow's main ally in the Arab world. While a treaty of friendship and co-operation exists between the two, the relationship is somewhat ambivalent, with Syria, while treasuring its special relationship with the Soviet Union, keeping a mind of its own. When Syria was contemplating sending its troops into Lebanon during the civil war there in the mid-1970s the Soviet Foreign Minister, Mr Kosygin, flew to Damascus to try to dissuade them. While he was still in the Syrian capital President Assad gave the order to move in. As one Western diplomat in Damascus told me: 'The Syrians feel the Russians need them more than they need the Russians. The Soviet Union must take what Damascus dishes out.' Joseph Sisco agrees: 'President Assad is dependent on the Soviet Union, but he is unlikely to become a total hostage.' And for the time being there's no sign that the relationship is under any serious strain with an estimated 4000 Russian advisers working in Syria.

Lebanon has been perhaps the most testing issue for President Assad. Without doubt Syria is keen to see Lebanon placed firmly under its wing, having openly backed the Muslim opposition groups which brought down the government in Beirut that had the backing of the United States and had signed a troop withdrawal agreement with Israel ('a second Camp David', as the Syrians called it). Within months, the Americans, humiliated by their attempts to impose their stamp on Lebanon and having lost more than 240 marines in a single suicide bombing, were forced to pull out of Beirut. And Syria's triumph was completed when the agreement between Lebanon and Israel was abrogated almost a year to the day after it had been signed. Since then, however, the going has not been easy. A number of security and political reform agreements have been hammered out by Lebanese leaders in Damascus, but none has lasted more than a year or so. The Lebanese quagmire looks as if it could drag the Syrians down as it did the Israelis and the Americans before them. And while Syria keeps some 30 000 troops in northern and eastern Lebanon, it is as reluctant to commit them to Beirut again as it did up to the Israeli invasion of 1982. Experience has shown that getting out of Beirut is much harder than getting in.

The traumatic experience of the United States in Lebanon should have taught Washington a lesson: dislike Syria and its policies if you will; accuse it of harbouring international terrorists and encouraging acts of terror; slate it for being an ally of the Soviet Union and Iran; say whatever you like, but ignore it at your peril.

In short, President Assad has manoeuvred Syria in such a way that it cannot be ignored whenever the major issues of the region are discussed. When Egypt was removed from the centre of the Arab stage after it signed the treaty with Israel, Syria was determined to take its place. It has a pivotal position in the Arab–Israel issue, as we've seen. It has too in the Gulf War. Syria supports the Iranians partly because of the rivalry between President Assad and Iraqi President Saddam Hussein, and partly because Syria receives oil from Iran at special prices. But in any event, Syria is the only Arab state with direct access to the leadership in Tehran, so if a day came when mediation was possible, Syria would be the only country in a position to carry it out. Already it has been ferrying messages to Tehran from the Gulf states. On the question of the future of the PLO, too, the Syrians have made sure that there can be no solution without their agreement, having backed a wing of the movement which is hostile to the PLO Chairman and is now based in Damascus. Once again, President Assad is determined that the PLO should not be tempted to join peace negotiations.

Such an ambitious role as Syria sees for itself needs plenty of financing, and it is not a rich country. It depends in large measure on aid from the oil-rich states, but with the recession in the Gulf most states which in 1978 promised financial support have stopped paying (some reports say only Saudi Arabia is still providing assistance). Syria has rich agricultural lands, being situated in the heart of the fertile crescent. A dam has been built on the Euphrates river to help irrigation; but with so much emphasis in the past on the military and on developing manufacturing industries, many acres of the rich farmland are under-used.

Some hopes lie in oil – three small fields have been producing small quantities of poor-quality crude for some years, nearly all of which is exported. Now, though, a new and much more promising field has been discovered in the eastern deserts of the country.

Tourism too is under-exploited. Some Iranians come these days to visit a Shiite shrine near Damascus; but you see few foreign visitors in the Suq – one of the most interesting in the region and containing the street called Straight, as mentioned in the Bible – or at the magnificent Ummayad mosque. And it's the same story too at other sites like the Krak des Chevaliers and Palmyra, or at one of the last villages in the world where Aramaic, the language spoken by Jesus, can still be heard. I get the impression that Syria will one day get round to developing a full-scale tourist industry. For the time being, though, President Assad has got plenty of other more important things on his mind.

For the average Syrian (Sunni, Alawite, Christian or Jew) austerity is beginning to bite, especially as President Assad has cracked down on what was a thriving smuggling business, with food, drink, consumer goods and luxury items coming in from Lebanon. Such products, not normally available because of a shortage of foreign exchange, were eagerly sought after by the relatively affluent middle class. Their absence is likely to anger a good proportion of the country. But again, President Assad will not be too troubled by that. He has shown that he deals toughly with those who stand up to him.

Syria hit the headlines in 1986 when Britain broke off diplomatic relations with Damascus. At a trial in London the Syrian Ambassador was found to have been implicated in a plot to try to blow up an Israeli airliner in mid-air on its way from London to Tel Aviv. The Syrians rigorously denied the charges. I was in Damascus as British diplomats left. Despite long tirades against Britain and British policies in the government-controlled media, there was no sign of animosity among ordinary Syrians who seemed more mystified and saddened than angered by the turn in events.

7 The Gulf States

Ancient traditions, modern wealth

Scattered pin-pricks of orange flame in the blackness far below. An occasional cluster of white lights, then fingers of lights marking the jetties stretching into the blackened sea and, further out, the splodges of light where the tankers are loading. It's a view from an airliner at night which is familiar to the hundreds of thousands of foreigners who have flown into the Gulf countries, drawn by the magnet of work and high wages which accompanied the oil boom. That view from the plane tells you a lot about the region – the oil-wells on and offshore with the gas being flared off, the lonely dots of civilisation in vast tracts of emptiness which by day amount to seemingly endless miles of khaki-brown sand, broken occasionally by a needle-thin line of an oil pipeline or a cross-desert road.

We are talking about a truly vast area of the world. Saudi Arabia, by far the biggest, richest and most influential Gulf country, is almost twice as large as the combined areas of Great Britain, France, West Germany and Italy. Furthermore the Gulf is an area with only tiny populations. Thus the extraordinary phenomenon of the oil boom which turned these states (by contrast, some of them are very small in area as well as population) into the richest countries – measured by income per head of the population – in the world. And to clear up a matter of terminology by 'Gulf states', we are talking, apart from Saudi Arabia, of Kuwait, the United Arab Emirates, Bahrain, Oman and Qatar.

And it all happened so fast. Looking at family photograph albums, I see pictures taken by my parents in 1959 of the centre of Abu Dhabi, showing camels wandering among the few low, crumbling stone buildings. Or of the same period, pictures of a banquet being prepared in the sandy yard of one of the first houses built in Abu Dhabi to celebrate the opening of the first foreign bank, the British Bank of the Middle East. The sheep for the banquet had been brought down from Dubai. Guest of honour was the former Ruler of Abu Dhabi, Sheikh Shakhbout, who had been persuaded to stop keeping his personal fortune under his bed and start putting it instead into banks. The era that was dawning then must have been impossible to imagine, the era of the strings of international luxury hotels and modern banks. A photograph of Dubai airport taken by my father as late as 1963 shows one solitary aircraft standing in the desert; today Dubai airport is one of the busiest in the world handling more than forty airlines. My father spoke of an occasion when the pilot of one of the small airlines that used to fly the routes connecting the lower Gulf states called him to the cockpit to help to locate Dubai airport. Peering groundwards, they eventually located the lines of oil drums that marked the flattened sand runway.

It happened so fast that I can't help feeling it could all end fast too. The talk in the Gulf these days is of recession. The consumer boom is over, the days of vast lucrative contracts for foreign companies are over; the emphasis today is on belt-tightening. Many of these oil states give an impression of, literally, being built on sand, with their small indigenous populations and their lack of an advanced social fabric which most other countries in the Arab world have. Already many of the once magnificent buildings in the region have lost their glitter; a few years of neglect under the fierce sun and in the heavy humidity, combined with the sandstorms which cover all in front of them as quickly and effectively as floodwater, and the region could look back on the mid- and late-twentieth century as one does on a dream.

This may be something of an exaggeration. But the phenomenon of the oil boom was the phenomenon of the twentieth century with all its trappings being imposed overnight on what were essentially desert people. The oil money brought the trappings, but it also paid for the labour to install them and the expertise to run them. You could spend a few days in Saudi Arabia, for example, without ever meeting a Saudi: your taxi driver might be from the Philippines, your hotel staff from Pakistan, your business contact from Egypt. The dilemma for these traditional Arab states has always been to gauge how far Western influences should be absorbed along with the tangible signs of Western society.

Saudi Arabia

The problem for Saudi Arabia, since it is both the richest and most traditional Gulf state, is probably greater than elsewhere in the Gulf. By tradition, the Saudi court moves out of the sunbaked desert capital of Riyadh during the Muslim fasting month of Ramadan. The princes and their entourages prefer to spend the hottest

months in the hill-top town of Taif, 100 miles inland from the Red
Sea Port of Jeddah, where the air is comparatively cool. The drive
there from Jeddah takes you towards the holy city of Mecca, the
birthplace of the Prophet Muhammad and the focus of prayer and
pilgrimage for the millions of Muslims throughout the world. As
you speed along the eight-lane highway, before a point where all
non-Muslims are required to take a right-hand fork to by-pass the
city, huge advertising signs compete for the pilgrim's attention,
offering Swiss and Japanese watches, electronic equipment,
teabags and much more. A non-Muslim is not allowed to visit
Mecca, but he can watch the evening prayers from there live on
Saudi television. And that's what appears so puzzling: the roots of
Islam wrapped in modern consumerism and technology. A traditional Arab society continuing in the most modern, and at times
the most futuristic, setting.

One cannot fail to be impressed by the development. It is truly
astonishing, and much of it very beautiful. Riyadh airport, as just
one example, is palatial, with its four huge domed terminals, the
light and airy decor inside enhanced by fountains and greenery.
One terminal is set aside for royalty and VIPs. When the British
Foreign Secretary, Sir Geoffrey Howe, was received there during a
Gulf tour early in 1986 the entourage went up the red carpet from

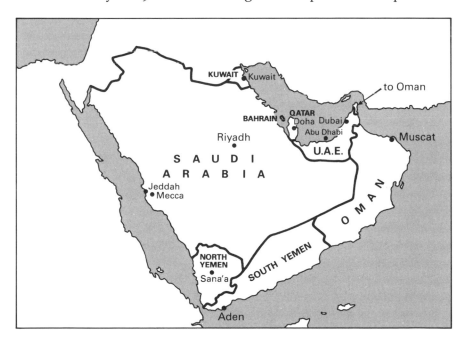

the steps of the plane into a large open room with a single Persian carpet covering the floor and gold adornments flowing down from the ceiling. Few airports can ever have offered such luxury. A subsidised internal air service links most of the major towns and cities, complementing the huge network of roads. There is plenty of water and electricity, the phones work well, there are modern hospitals and universities, and shops are stocked as well as any in the world. In fact, they have anything that money can buy.

That is the point: the Saudis have been able quite simply to buy the best in the world, including adornments like the soaring Geneva-style fountain at Jeddah. Saudis have also been able to buy an expatriate community sufficiently big to run everything. Informed estimates put the number of foreigners at three to four million, probably not far short of the total number of Saudis (population figures here, as elsewhere in the Gulf, vary considerably). Over the past year or so, because of the big drop in oil revenues, there has been a sharp reduction in the number of foreigners working in the Kingdom. This has been partly caused by natural wastage, with the big labour-intensive projects coming to an end, but it is partly deliberate policy to save money. At the beginning of 1986 regulations were introduced greatly restricting the movement of foreigners between jobs in the Kingdom.

Nevertheless, there is still a very substantial expatriate community in Saudi Arabia and there will have to be one there for decades to come. For while moves are under way to trim the foreign workforce by about half a million, the truth is that the Saudis themselves do not show much inclination to take over most of the jobs, particularly the inferior ones. So, again, it's puzzling how the Saudis can maintain a traditional society, not just with the trappings of a modern one all round, but with such a large presence of foreigners from so many different societies.

The Saudi answer seems to be to allow as little overlap as possible between their society and those of the expatriates. Even foreigners who have lived in the Kingdom for a long time say they find it almost impossible to enter deep friendships with the Saudis. One long-serving foreign ambassador who was an outspoken friend of the Kingdom was dismayed when only one Saudi attended a party to mark his departure.

The members of the foreign community live apart and are tolerated on certain conditions. Few allowances are made for them. For example, while Christians are allowed to work in the country, they are not allowed to worship. Churches are banned. And as it is often reported, the consumption of alcohol is not allowed, women are forbidden to drive, and religious police, with formidable powers, are on hand to check that foreign women do not dress with their legs and arms bare. And in what is regarded by many diplomats as a move to isolate further the foreign communities, all embassies were ordered in 1985 to move from the cosmopolitan and relatively liberal atmosphere of Jeddah, to a diplomatic compound just outside the clean but, for me, soul-less modern city of Riyadh.

To talk of recession in Saudi Arabia is of course relative. This is because at the height of the oil boom the Kingdom was producing ten million barrels a day and receiving a high price for it. Within a few years, production had dropped to two million barrels a day and prices had slumped. That might have been catastrophic news for many oil producers. But the change was cushioned for the Saudis by the secure and comforting knowledge that they have beneath their deserts a quarter of the world's oil reserves. The boom, when it came, was sensational even by Gulf standards. Now it's a question of belt-tightening, getting rid of the extra car, keeping the old one a little longer than in the past and getting into a frame of mind which accepts that the days of unlimited growth and unlimited profit are gone. The Saudis admit that at times they allowed themselves to be overcharged by the foreign companies that came greedily for a share of the riches. But as one senior official told me: 'We got things more expensively than we might have done; but we wanted to get things done quickly.' And the Saudis console themselves with the thought that all the major infrastructure has been laid down and paid for. Now Saudi Arabia must learn to live more (and I stress more) like a normal country, lowering slightly its expectations.

The Gulf states as a whole in the end will probably benefit from the fact that they have small indigenous populations, whose demands can be met for the foreseeable future by a combination of continuing oil exports and big financial reserves deposited overseas. Major unrest, therefore, is not thought to be likely. For such 'working class' as there is tends to be foreign and therefore can be expelled at the first hint of trouble.

That's not to say, though, that there will not be pressure – for example, from young Saudis who have studied abroad and return to a society that at its roots has changed little from the days of September 1932 when Ibn Saud founded the Kingdom, where there was an observance of a very strict interpretation of Sunni Islam, where traditional punishments were still applied, where women never appeared in public. For a young Saudi who has spent three years in Europe or the United States, returning to such a closed society where even cinemas are banned might seem like an intolerable hardship. There are some who would like to see a more tolerant society, but not many. And in fact, such major trouble as there has been has, perhaps ironically, come from Muslim fundamentalists who believed that the Kingdom was becoming too liberal. The incident that shocked Saudi Arabia and the whole region most of all was the siege of the Grand Mosque in Mecca in November 1979 by fundamentalists who believed that the Saudi authorities were debasing Islam. The siege was ended only after Saudi troops stormed the building leaving many people dead.

But Saudi society itself seems secure enough to withstand these kinds of pressures. For unlike any other country in the Middle East, Saudi Arabia is an indigenous Arab and Islamic state. The great fourteenth-century Arab historian and intellectual, Ibn Khaldoun, wrote about the importance in society of what is known as *asabiyya* – the sense of mutual affection and willingness to fight and die for each other, a kind of tribal solidarity. There is still a strong sense of asabiyya among the ruling Saudi family in the late twentieth century. And it's a way of life that seems to satisfy most Saudis. Many say they wish there was more freedom of expression and more democracy. But as one Saudi prince told me: 'We would find it impolite to attack God, the King or the country. Some newly educated middle-class Saudis might like a bit more in the way of basic democratic freedoms. But it isn't something that bothers us all that much. We certainly don't wake up in the morning worrying about it.'

As elsewhere in the Gulf, the main platform for grievances to be aired is at the traditional *majlis* where even the most senior members of society hold open house and will receive anyone who wishes to be heard. The Saudis believe that in this way they can keep in touch with the currents in society in a way that suits their style of living much more than access through the ballot box would. 'The more senior you get, the more ordinary people you meet,' was how one official put it. For another thing, the Saudis (and the other Gulf Arabs) do not have a habit of taking decisions quickly, in the way that people in the West traditionally do. 'The style of reaching decisions,' a prince told me, 'takes longer with us, it requires consensus – almost by telepathy.'

The royal family in Saudi Arabia keeps in touch with the thinking in the country also by virtue of the fact that it is so big. Ibn Saud, who died in 1953, had more than forty sons; today there are reckoned to be as many as 5000 princes (as one of them joked: 'You know what we say: we have more princes than taxi drivers'). The princes, depending on their merit and education, hold a very large number of the top jobs in government, industry and the armed forces. They are in fact a ready-made information-gathering network.

Saudi society is much criticised – in private inside the Arab world, and more publicly outside it – for being based on double standards. Examples of excesses by Saudi princes and businessmen abroad are highlighted by foreign newspapers. But the Saudis themselves argue that this is the behaviour of a tiny minority being given exaggerated coverage. And they bitterly resent Western criticism of the way they run their country – hence the anger they displayed when British television viewers in 1980 were shown *Death of a Princess*, a film about the execution of a Saudi princess for adultery. They believe that they have in fact succeeded where other Arab countries have failed in coping with the twentieth century. In these countries, they argue, the wholesale assimilation of Western morals has tended to create tensions and has generally led to the rejection of those morals. Saudi Arabia, the guardian of the holy cities of Islam (Mecca and Medina), may be packaged in Western dressings, but has been constantly Arab and Islamic.

A considerable amount of time is devoted by those who rule Saudi Arabia to regional matters. This is often misinterpreted as the Saudis trying to exert regional influence because they are the leading regional paymasters, providing support for the Palestine Liberation Organisation and Syria, for example. In fact, they are trying to make use of this influence to bring the Arab countries together. It is not their style to try to force one group or another to adopt or drop a particular policy by threatening to cut off funds. Rather, the Saudis, who are conservative and cautious by nature, try to stand back from regional controversies, the intention being to mend, rather than widen splits within the Arab world; for a simple reason. As one senior government official told me: 'We want less conflict in the countries round about us. In the long run we want peace and quiet.' So it was that in the late 1970s when

President Sadat of Egypt began talks with Israel, Saudi Arabia, while deploring Sadat, went out of her way to prevent action being taken against Egypt until the last minute; the hope was that the President could be persuaded to change his mind and thus prevent the further fragmentation of the Arab world.

Saudi Arabia is anxious that no regional turmoil should upset the flow of its oil abroad, and that no conflict should allow the Soviet Union to gain in influence in the region. The Saudis are fiercely anti-communist. While there have been hints, for example, that the Kingdom might establish diplomatic relations with the Soviet Union, foreign diplomats think this is highly unlikely while Russian troops remain in Afghanistan (a Muslim country).

Without question the greatest threat to stability in the Gulf region comes from the long-running war between Iran and Iraq (see Chapter 8). The Saudis, because of their dislike of the revolutionary fervour of the Shiites in Iran, support the Iraqis; but, again in the interests of stability, they've made diplomatic contact with the Iranians from time to time to see if a solution could be found.

GCC

The outbreak of the Gulf War was the catalyst for the formation of the organisation called the Gulf Co-operation Council (GCC), the other members besides Saudi Arabia being Bahrain, Kuwait, Oman, Qatar and the United Arab Emirates (UAE). As in all regional units in the Arab world, there are many similarities between the various member states as well as many differences. It's perhaps going too far to say that the GCC is motivated by the slogan 'united we stand, divided we fall,' for the individual states do not look like falling, whether by political, economic or military disasters. But it is true that threats to the stability of the area have concentrated the minds of the six member states in a way that hardly seemed possible when the Council was created in the aftermath of the Iranian revolution. The revolution, of course, brought down the Shah (who regarded his country as the policeman of the Gulf) and caused the subsequent instability in the region. The GCC has confounded the toughest sceptics simply by surviving. Now, even they are having to concede that progress is being made towards greater co-operation, albeit so far on a limited scale.

The threat of the Shiite revolution spilling over into the Gulf states has always been a fear. While the Gulf countries are predominantly Sunni muslim, there are Shiite communities in eastern

Saudi Arabia, in Bahrain (where well over half the population is Shiite) and in Kuwait (where around a quarter is). In Bahrain, a pro-Iranian coup attempt was foiled in 1981. This threat took on much more dramatic proportions with the prolonging of the Gulf War and the reversals which Iraq suffered after its earlier successes. And the war was brought to the doorsteps of the Gulf states in 1984 when both countries involved started attacking shipping in the Gulf, thus seriously threatening the oil supplies to the West and the lifeblood of the states themselves. As the Iraqis struck at tankers collecting Iranian oil, the Iranians hit back at Arab-owned shipping and ships using Arab ports (see p. 120). The result was not in the end a serious disruption to the export of oil from the Gulf states, but it made insurance rates soar, and had the effect of deterring shipping coming into the Gulf, thus cutting down the work and therefore the earnings in the ports and dry-docks. All this added to the effects of the recession.

In 1984 too, the Saudi airforce shot down an Iranian fighter which had entered Saudi airspace, and a major escalation in tension seemed to be on the cards. However, both states – perhaps realising the danger – played down the incident. But the threat to oil supplies to the United States and other Western countries, combined with the Iranian threat to block the Straits of Hormuz at the entrance to the Gulf, prompted Washington to send AWACS reconnaissance jets to Saudi Arabia. And at various times during the day and night, Riyadh shakes with the roar of these planes and the huge in-flight refuelling jets taking off and landing.

To cope with these threats, the GCC has been busy trying to co-ordinate its defences, holding joint military manoeuvres and set-ting up a rapid deployment force, with all the states contributing, based in Saudi Arabia. This is little more than a token force at the moment, but it has given the GCC a cohesion which it never had before.

The GCC had been founded first and foremost as an economic organisation, and in this field some progress has been made on such matters as customs duty and insurance regulations. What is needed, though, is better co-ordination on sharing resources in the face of the current recession. For in the boom days, all the states wanted all the prestige symbols of development, such as lavish airports, dry-docks, fertiliser plants and so on. There was enor-mous overlap and duplication; and enormous waste.

The Emirates

This duplication of resources can be seen in one of the lower Gulf states, the United Arab Emirates (UAE) which was formed in December 1971 when Britain withdrew its armed forces from the Gulf and cut political ties which had given Britain the controlling hand in many of the states. British influence in the area dates back to the early nineteenth century when its merchant ships came under frequent attack from pirates in Ras al-Khaimah and other places in the lower Gulf giving the region the name 'The Pirate Coast'. Britain first used force to try to defeat the pirates, then concluded a series of treaties with the sheikhs in what was thereafter known as the 'Trucial Coast'. Britain watched over the region through the eyes of a Political Agent in Dubai who reported to the Political Resident in Bahrain. In the 1950s Sharjah, on the coast near Dubai, was the base for a force known as the Trucial Oman Scouts which was led by British officers, and later Sharjah became a base for the Royal Air Force. When Britain withdrew, six emirates (principalities) from the 'Trucial Coast' became federated to form the UAE. They were: Abu Dhabi, Dubai, Sharjah, Ajman, Umm al-Quwain and Fujeirah. Later Ras al-Khaimah was to join too.

In theory the seven emirates pool their resources and work under a federal government. In practice, though, Abu Dhabi, because its oil revenue has made it by far the richest of the emirates, is effectively the paymaster. The relationship between the seven has not always been easy, and the individual emirates have not always supported the federal idea with as much enthusiasm as might have been hoped for. The highest body of the UAE is the Supreme Council of Rulers – the seven Emirs. At the end of 1985 they met for just two hours; this was their first meeting for a year and a half. And coming back to the subject of airports, a country with a population of something just over one million has five, all of international standard, and another two are being built. While Dubai, with its much sought-after duty free shop, handles more than forty airlines, an international timetable in March 1986 showed that Sharjah airport, just miles up the road, handled only seven flights a week, and under Ras al-Khaimah airport 50 miles further up the coast, only three flights were listed.

Much of the rivalry has been between Abu Dhabi and Dubai. For Dubai is the one city with a long history; some of the square wind towers, relics of the days before air conditioning and electric fans, can still be seen among the tall modern buildings. Dubai feels like an established city. It's built around a wide creek, the quays of which bustle with activity, and the dhows load and unload their goods as they have done for decades – everything from gold watches to cement or goats. For while Dubai is also an oil producer (production began in 1969), it is above all else a city that thrives on trade of every kind and had a reputation of being the smuggling centre of the Gulf. The city has a cosmoplitan feel to it quite unlike any other in the Gulf. Much of the trade is with Iran, for despite the Gulf War there is still an Iranian community in Dubai and there are direct flights to Tehran.

One of the most glaring differences between the seven emirates concerns the federal defence force. Dubai has never contributed to the force, as all the other emirates have. Instead it has its own force, entirely self-financed, with the misleading title of the Central Military Command of the UAE Army. Other emirates too, in particular Sharjah and Ras al-Khaimah, are strengthening their own forces under the pretext that they are intended for internal security. Sharjah has bought its own tanks, and arms dealers say there is a considerable amount of business within the various emirates.

Oman

The Gulf state with the closest links with Britain is Oman on the eastern shore of the peninsula. In appearance, Oman is spectacular, much of its hinterland made up of impenetrable, craggy and arid mountains, while in the south the soil is watered from May to September by monsoon rains. Only from the air can one appreciate the beauty of the country which until 1970 had been one of the most isolated and backward in the world. Viewed from a helicopter the grey mountains contrast with the azure, unpolluted waters of the Indian Ocean. On a visit once with the British Foreign Secretary we flew up to the Jebel Akhdar (green mountain), a plateau 6000 feet above sea level where vegetation grows on small steppes. The Omani Army has a camp there now; but in the late 1950s it was the remote hideaway of an Imam who was challenging the authority of the Sultan in Muscat. It was the British Special Air Service (SAS) which, responding to a request from the Sultan, conquered the terrain, reached the plateau and succeeded in flushing out the rebels.

This was an era when, while the rest of the Arab world was experiencing the fruits of twentieth-century development, Oman was scarcely even peeping through the window of that century, the curtains being kept drawn by Sultan Said bin Taimur. He was eventually deposed, with help from the British, by his son, Sultan Qabous, who rules Oman today. When he took over from his father he was faced with a country where there was little electricity, three schools for the whole country with a population at that time of something up to a million or so and only six miles of tarmacked road. The old Sultan ruled with a rod of iron, forbidding travel in or out of Muscat after nightfall and insisting that anyone who ventured out in the capital after dark should carry a lantern. In 1985, Oman celebrated the fifteenth anniversary of the accession of Sultan Qabous. It was seen as a coming-of-age party. And the transformation has been sensational. With the revenue from oil (Oman produces just over half a million barrels each day and like Britain and Norway is not a member of OPEC) the Omanis have built an elaborate and impressive infrastructure. Schools and hospitals have sprung up around the country, and a university has recently opened.

Not all the oil revenue by any means, though, is available for development. Defence is one of the most important considerations for the Omanis; Sultan Qabous was trained at Sandhurst and heads one of the most respected armed forces in the region with the assistance of some 200 British officers on loan from the United Kingdom and about 1000 men on contract.

Until the mid 1970s the chief concern of the Sultan's army was to put down a left-wing rebellion in Dhofar province in the south of the country. Insurgents operating from neighbouring South Yemen, and with the backing of Aden, were trying to bring down the sultanate. With the help of Iranian (Iran was then under the Shah), Jordanian and Pakistani men and equipment, and operating in extremely difficult conditions which suited the insurgent more than the defending troops, the rebellion was eventually squashed. An amnesty was granted, and two former opponents of the government in Muscat are now in the cabinet.

For the time being, the future looks promising for Oman. Unlike the rest of the Gulf it is still enjoying economic and commercial expansion, and has benefited from careful planning, managing to avoid some of the excesses witnessed in other Gulf states. There is a very strict control on who is allowed into the country, but inside it feels relaxed. And while motorways tear past the old walled city of Muscat, the Sultan has been trying to keep the traditional and unique atmosphere of this most easterly Arab state. The men, for example, still wear the smart white full-length robe which is known as the *dishdasha*, with traditional crescent-shaped silver daggers called *Khanjars* tucked into their belts and turbans wound around their heads.

One possible cloud on the horizon concerns the succession. Sultan Qabous has no heir. So one of his tasks will be to prepare for a peaceful handover of power when that becomes necessary.

The main military concern today for Oman is the Gulf War. Oman controls the northern finger of the peninsula which reaches up into the Straits of Hormuz, the 24-mile wide strip of water at the entrance to the Gulf through which so much of the West's oil passes on board tankers. The Omanis don't believe the Iranians are capable of blocking the straits as they've threatened. But they see it as their job to police the waters, making sure tankers stick to their allotted lanes. Also the Omanis try to prevent the Iranian navy stopping ships to search them to see if they are carrying arms or equipment for Iraq.

Kuwait

The Gulf War is the major concern these days too for Kuwait, the northernmost Gulf state and neighbour of Iraq. The fighting over the past year or two has come dangerously close to Kuwaiti soil. In 1981, oil installations near the Iraqi border were attacked by Iranian jets. During Iranian land offensives close to Basra, the sound of fighting can be heard in Kuwait, a chilling reminder (if one were needed) of how close the war has come to spilling out of the current battlefields. The Kuwaitis have been alarmed too by the attacks on shipping since vessels flying the Kuwaiti flag have been among those hit.

Equally alarming has been the sense of insecurity within Kuwait related to the neighbouring conflict. In December 1983 the city of Kuwait was the scene of a string of bomb attacks against the United States and French Embassies, and a number of government targets. These were apparently motivated by Kuwait's support of Iraq in the war. A group believed to have connections with Iraqi Shiite opposition, known as Islamic Jihad, said it was behind the bombings. A number of men were later arrested and sentenced to death, but the sentences have never been carried out. In the aftermath of the bombing about 600 non-Kuwaiti Arab workers and other foreigners considered potentially troublesome were sent home. But more was to come. In May 1985 the Emir of Kuwait,

Shiekh Jaber al-Ahmad al-Sabah, escaped alive when a car bomb attack was directed at his motorcade. And later in the year, bombs exploded in two crowded cafés.

Kuwait is one of the classic and much quoted stories of rags-to-riches success following the discovery of oil. The original settlement of Kuwait was founded in the middle of the eighteenth century by tribesmen from the heart of the Arabian desert who had come looking for water and grazing land for their flocks. The Sabah family have been dominant from that time. Over the following century, while the Kuwaitis paid lip service to the Ottoman Empire, they established close links with Britain. For the British, Kuwait was an important communications and trade link. In 1899 Britain and Kuwait signed an agreement giving London control of Kuwaiti foreign policy. This was scrapped in 1961 when Kuwait became independent, but the British were still to play a role. For a month or so later the Emir called for British military help after Iraq claimed Kuwait as part of its territory. British troops landed in the sweltering summer heat, but their stay was brief because a joint Arab force was quickly assembled to replace them.

The oil industry, which for the past decades has dominated life in Kuwait, came into being before the Second World War. Not until the 1950s and '60s, though, did it transform Kuwait from a small coastal town making its living by trade, by building and pearl fishing, into one of the world's leading oil-producing countries. And more than that, into one of the most prosperous and generous welfare states in the region.

Kuwait today has the most solid feel of any of the modern cities built with oil money. It is also a city full of energy, boasting one of the most lively and respected local presses in the Arab world. It has an active university, and political and cultural life is stimulated unlike anywhere else in the Gulf by the presence of a Palestinian community of some 300 000 people.

Furthermore, Kuwait stands apart from its Gulf neighbours by having an elected National Assembly. Parliamentary life has not always been smooth: only native born Kuwaitis are allowed to vote (a fraction of the population of 1.5–2 million); the parliament has been accused of obstructing legislation and for four years parliamentary life was suspended.

But the Assembly does provide a healthy platform for the issues of the day to be discussed, something that is missing in the other Gulf states.

Bahrain

The island state of Bahrain (in fact an archipelago of more than thirty islands) to the south of Kuwait and sitting just off the shores of Saudi Arabia, followed the Kuwaiti experiment for a while. Two years after independence in 1971, a National Assembly was set up. The following year, though, saw industrial unrest sparked off by rising prices and delays in the formation of promised trade unions; and in 1975 the Prime Minister of the day resigned on the grounds that the parliament was hampering the job of government. The National Assembly was suspended by the Emir, and it has never reappeared.

Bahrain, by the nature of its geographical position, is as anxious as any of the Gulf states about the progress of the Gulf War. In 1984, at the start of the attacks on shipping, my colleagues and I hired a launch to go out to see an oil tanker damaged by an attack by Iranian jets in retaliation for a hit by Iraqi planes on a tanker using Kharg Island. The Bahrain authorities, while allowing us to report for their country, were as unhappy about the prospect of bad publicity damaging their reputation as a spot of tranquillity as they were about the threat of the warfare actually hitting their island.

For this is Bahrain's great attraction. It is the most liberal of all the Gulf states, possibly of all the Arab states. While an early producer of oil, it soon learned that it was never going to be one of the giants, so channelled its energies into service industries of every kind, as well as setting up an aluminium smelter. Communications with the outside world were always good, off-shore banking units were created, and the island – with its relaxed regulations on entertainments, including the provision of night-clubs and bars serving alcohol (the latter not to be found in Kuwait, Saudi Arabia or Qatar) – became a rest and recreation centre for Arabs and foreigners alike from the surrounding countries. Manama, the capital, is a city where you will find, for example, an Italian restaurant packed with foreigners clapping and singing along as the guitarist thumps out 'Viva España' and 'Guantanamera'; it's where you will find discotheques and wine bars – with perhaps an Englishman as host; it is where you are offered fish and chips in the Dilmoun bar and you can stop for a pint in the 'Sherlock Holmes' pub in the Gulf Hotel. The completion of a 15-mile causeway over the coral-bedded shallows between Bahrain and Saudi Arabia could increase the worth of this particular service industry although the postponement of its opening was brought about by delay in building up the access roads. However, some have argued that the delay was connected with fears on the part of the Bahrainis that, if the facility were to be abused, there might be an attempt by the Saudi authorities to crack down on the pleasures offered.

Bahrain, though, has the feel of an oasis. It is naturally green because of the existence of freshwater springs on and offshore. Furthermore the weather is unbearably humid in summer when all that is metal turns fast to rust. To step outside an air-conditioned room is like walking into a wall of heat with the smell of oil and gas from the refinery heavy on the air. It was mid-summer when I arrived for the first time in Bahrain in the late 1950s. My parents and I had flown from Beirut in a Viscount which had bumped its way through the turbulence which covered the sky over the vast and burning desert of Arabia. (One particular bump combined with the carelessness of a seven-year-old contrived to see me pouring a bottle of fizzy drink all over the man next to me. It turned out he was one of my father's chief customers.) In those days the island had a strong colonial feel, and the links with pre-independence India were noticeable. Apart from the presence of a very big community from the sub-continent, the rupee was still the currency. We lived in a huge house with balconies all around set in a lush garden with its own tennis court. In one corner of the garden there was a bush of pampas grass where a mongoose used to hide. And green parrots and hoopoes were regular visitors. Behind the house was a palm forest and a village of *barastis* – small houses made of interwoven dried palm fronds.

From this house every day the driver would take me in the blue Humber Hawk across the causeway to the small island of Muharraq where the airport is located and where in those days there was an RAF base. I attended the RAF school. It was an era when my parents were invited to the Queen's birthday celebrations on the lawns of the British Residence, a Political Resident rather than ambassador being Her Majesty's senior representative. At that time, the building overlooked the sea. Now it is surrounded by land reclaimed from the sea, an island of a bygone era.

Today Manama has a tower-block sky-line like all the other Gulf cities. On one occasion during the Muslim fasting month of Ramadan I was in a room high up in one of the luxury hotels watching the evening approach (again the hotel was standing on land which did not exist when I was a child). A distant boom from a big gun

Palestine Liberation Organisation leader Yasir Arafat, besieged in Tripoli, North Yemen after the PLO had been forced out of Beirut. BELOW *Following the massacre of Palestinians in the refugee camps of Sabra and Chatila in 1982, the International Red Cross supervise the removal and cremation of the victims' bodies.*

LEFT   *Beirut 1976. Soldiers of the Palestine Liberation Army patrol a buffer zone between enemy sections of the capital.* ABOVE   *The wrecked building of the US Embassy in Beirut, rammed by a vehicle packed with explosives on 18 April 1983.* BELOW   *A wounded militiaman of the Sunni Muslim Murabitoun is evacuated by his friends, following fighting in the Holiday Inn, Beirut 1976.*

Busy waterfront at Dubai; traditional sailing boats that ply the Gulf moor alongside buildings from more recent years. LEFT   The Dubai Trade Centre, UAE, towers above the expanse of near emptiness.

LEFT   A tribesman from the mountains of Oman, in traditional dress.
RIGHT   Contrasts in the Gulf styles: modern buildings dwarf the Old Tower of
Sharjah, UAE, though still retaining hints of Muslim architecture.
BELOW   The desert Bedouins, advance guard of the Saudi Arabian army.

Ships lying idle in the Shatt-al-Arab waterway, casualties of the Gulf War.
BELOW   An Iranian casualty in the seemingly endless Gulf War between Iran and
Iraq following the Iranian drive against the city of Basra; a picture of Ayatollah
Khomeini is taped to his pillar and he takes comfort in reading the Koran.

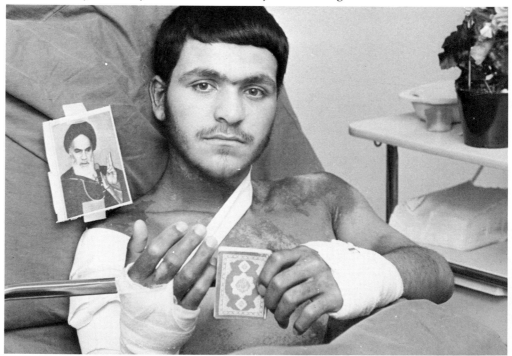

Following the funeral of twenty Libyans killed by the American bombing raid on Tripoli in April 1986, young and old alike demonstrate against President Reagan and chant anti-American slogans.
LEFT   Libyans survey the result of the USAF bombing raid on Tripoli, April 1986.

RIGHT   *Islamic architecture is illustrated by this gateway in the walled Moroccan city of Fez.*
BELOW   *Arab leaders meet in Tripoli, Libya, to condemn Egyptian President Sadat's overtures to Israel: Colonel Qadafi, President of Libya; Yasir Arafat, leader of the PLO; President Boumedienne of Algeria; and President Assad of Syria.*

announced sunset. One by one the muezzins all over the city began their calls. The island was covered in white mist, the sky and horizon were obscured by a sandstorm. And the stone buildings in that pale evening light took on the texture of marble. From my hotel I could see too the palm forests looking dusty and sad as the new buildings which replaced the barastis encroached further and further.

Qatar

The sixth of the states of the GCC is Qatar, that thumb of land pushing up into the Gulf, on the top of which floats Bahrain. Qatar is a quiet, comfortable and low-key state, large in area and small in population (not much more than a quarter of a million), eighty per cent of whom live in the capital, Doha. 'Qatar doesn't stick its nose into others' affairs: that's how it keeps out of trouble.' That was the assessment of a foreigner with many years of experience of the country. 'There are no great pressures: the Qataris are happy to go along at their own sweet pace.' Qatar is the quiet partner in the GCC.

Geographical, religious and family ties link Qatar closely to Saudi Arabia. The ruling Al-Thani family came originally from central Saudi Arabia. Both countries practise a conservative form of Islam and there has been considerable inter-marriage. The dwindling number of bedouin families regularly cross the joint border in search of pastures.

The Qatari economy is based on oil and oil products; reserves are reckoned to be good for another forty years or so. But Qatar has one major asset: the biggest concentration of untapped natural gas in the world. Like all the Gulf states Qatar has tried to diversify its economic base by investing in manufacturing industry, and a big industrial complex has been built at Umm Said south of Doha where the country's oil terminal is situated. However, Qatar is not exempt from the problems being faced by all the neighbouring states. The products (steel bar, fertilisers and cement) are intended for local markets where the demand has dried up because of the completion of most capital projects and the general recession. Once again, though, the indigenous population is incredibly small – the figure could be as low as 70–80 000. In the worst event, with the infrastructure completed and with a cushion of gas reserves, the Qataris will be left with fewer worries than most Arab states.

In the meantime the Qataris who – unlike some of their Gulf

colleagues – like to keep matters within their own hands rather than delegate them to foreigners, have been concentrating on improving the environment. The change has been dramatic. Since 1974 the capital, Doha, has been turned into one of the most pleasant cities in the Gulf with greenery providing shade from the fierce heat. The corniche, which is a favourite meeting place, is reckoned to be the most attractive in the Gulf. The contrast when you leave the city, though, is great and sudden with the trees and Islamic-style architecture giving way to inhospitable desert.

The Qataris also devote a lot of energy to traditional culture. The old palace in Doha has been converted into a folk museum, winning the Aga Khan award in 1979. Traditional bedouin poetry and folk-arts are encouraged. As one observer put it: 'More than any other Gulf Arabs, the Qataris are determined to keep their own identity.'

So against this troubling background of a war on their doorstep and economic recession at home, the Gulf states are having to shape up for an uncertain future. Neither issue is easy to ignore. At the time of writing Iraq was bracing itself for a new Iranian ground offensive. As many as one million Iranians were said to be massing on the border and the Tehran government has promised that this will provide the decisive breakthrough in this lengthy conflict. On the economic front there are signs that the price of oil might be on the rise again, giving hope that revenues will soon recover some of their strength. But it seems equally clear that the boom years, the spectacular period of unbridled expenditure – whether it was on soundly assessed development projects or rash flights of extravagance – were over. And as the foreign workers assemble their electronic goods and other booty from the years of opulence and gloat over their bank balances at home, the challenge to the Gulf Arabs is to work out how to play a full role in the region. And that will be achieved most successfully by making the Gulf Co-operation Council a voice to be respected and taken heed of. In turn, that won't happen unless the aspirations of the individual states are channelled much more towards the interests of the Gulf as a whole than they are at the moment.

8 The Gulf War

A forgotten conflict

It's being called the forgotten war. After over six years of conflict
the world has become bored with 'news of fresh fighting in the
Gulf War between Iran and Iraq.' For many people, though, it is by
no means forgotten – for example, for the families of those killed on
both sides. There is no reliable death list but one million dead for
Iran alone is now being widely quoted, even by the Iranians themselves. The war is not forgotten either by the governments of the
two countries, which pour millions of pounds into the war effort
and into coping with the financial hardships resulting from high
defence spending. And in addition the conflict is very much a top
concern for the Arab Gulf states, frightened that the war might spill
over into their territory and disrupt the tranquillity of the lower
Gulf.

Probably what is forgotten more than anything else is why the
war between these two countries (which have nearly 1000 miles of
common border) started in the first place. Two main explanations
are put forward; in all probability there is some truth in each of
them. One explanation is to do with disputed territory, the other
religion.

Iraq's second city of Basra lies on a waterway which marks the
border between that country and Iran. It was once a thriving port,
with the waterway – known as the Shatt al-Arab – carrying ships
back and forth from the Gulf some 40 miles away. The waterway
was, in fact, Iraq's only access to the sea. Today, the Shatt al-Arab
is still full of shipping. But the vessels have been there since 22
September 1980 when the war with Iran began. These rusting ships
(according to maritime sources there are more than seventy),
looked at through a screen of palm trees which borders the Shatt
al-Arab in Basra, symbolise the stagnation of the whole conflict.
Basra itself, stripped of its role as a port city, lies as if in mourning,
cocooned in thousands, probably millions of sandbags to protect it
against the frequent artillery and air attacks from the Iranians.

Basra has had more experience of the war than any other population centre in Iraq. It lies close to the Iranian front line, making it

an obvious target. Staying in a hotel on the edge of the Shatt al-Arab in 1985 I was woken in the early hours by the shriek of shells passing over the building and exploding just behind it. A few minutes later the city's air raid sirens wailed, a sound familiar in the cities of both Iraq and Iran. For the population of Basra it was just another barrage, and in fact it had been expected. On the previous day Iraqi jets had hit at a number of Iranian cities. This was the ritual reply. It caused minimal damage and few casualties. But it was just enough to keep the people of Basra reminded of the war that won't go away.

Early this century, in 1913, Iran (then Persia) and Turkey (Iraq was then part of the Ottoman Empire) agreed that their common border in this area should be defined as running down the centre of the Shatt al-Arab waterway. In 1937, though, this agreement was superseded by a treaty which passed sovereignty of the waterway over to Iraq. By the late 1960s it was the turn of the Iranians to be dissatisfied: they sought a renegotiation of the joint agreement. Iraq refused.

Another complicating factor in the background to the outbreak of war was the Kurdish problem. The Kurds are a transnational ethnic group living in the Taurus mountains of eastern Anatolia and north-western Iran. They are spread therefore throughout Turkey, Iraq and Iran (and beyond), but in spite of a strong historic sense of independence and a long-standing reputation for military prowess, nowhere have they achieved political autonomy. During the 1960s and '70s the Iraqi government put a great deal of effort in terms of manpower, military equipment and money into trying to subdue rebellions by the Kurdish community in the north of the country who were fighting for independence. By 1974 the fighting had got to such a pitch that the Iraqis were forced to step up considerably the military campaign. Many of the Kurds fled into neighbouring Iran, and those that survived could continue fighting only with help from Iran.

Relations between Iraq and Iran at this time were strained, in large part because of the Kurdish issue. There were some minor border clashes and a heated propaganda war. Then occurred one of those amazing political surprises that the Middle East is capable of producing from time to time. Vice president Saddam Hussein of Iraq (the current President) and the Shah of Iran, while in Algiers in March 1975 for a meeting of petroleum exporting countries (OPEC), agreed to end their border disputes, stop subversive

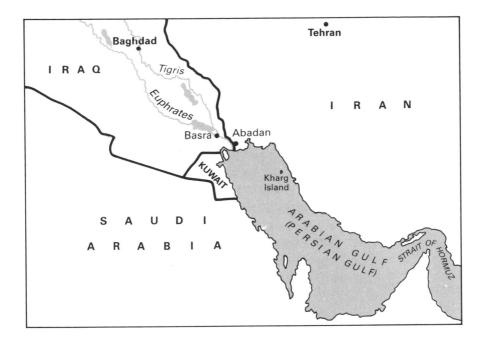

activity in each other's affairs and return to the original agreement on the Shatt al-Arab which defined the border as running up the middle of the waterway. It was classic Middle East bargaining: Iraq gave in to Iran's wishes on the question of the Shatt al-Arab; in return, Iran promised to cut off aid to the Kurds in Iraq. Almost immediately the Kurdish rebellion was over.

Matters might have stayed thus had the Shah not been deposed in 1979 to be replaced by the Shiite Muslim revolutionary leader Ayatollah Khomeini. Whether it was intended as a pretext for launching the war or not, in the autumn of the following year, Iraq accused Iran of failing to implement fully the terms of the agreement signed in Algiers, and demanded the removal of Iranian forces from a border position. Iran shrugged off the demand. The Baghdad government promptly abrogated the Algiers agreement, and on 22 September 1980 the Gulf War began. It began on a grand scale that was to foreshadow the horrifying proportions of the whole conflict. The Iraqi forces opened up a 300-mile battle front as they advanced into Iranian territory. To their surprise, however, they met fierce Iranian resistance; within months it was clear that neither side was going to win a quick or easy victory.

Why, then, did President Saddam Hussein commit himself to the war? On the face of it, a dispute over borders would not seem to justify such a big military operation. Even if it did, the Iraqis clearly misjudged their opposition. Whatever the motive, it seems beyond doubt that President Saddam Hussein was counting on a short, sharp operation that would cost few lives and give a boost to his own prestige within Iraq.

Most people now believe that the Iraqi intention was far broader than simply to stamp out border friction. Rather, the military operation was intended to bring down the revolutionary leadership in Tehran. Since the revolution, Iraq had been deeply mistrustful of the Iranians' intentions for two reasons: first, the openly declared intention of the Tehran government to encourage Muslims in neighbouring countries to follow Iran's example and work for an Islamic revolution; and, second, the fact that more than half the population of Iraq are Shiite Muslims and might therefore provide rich soil for the seeds of revolution and thus threaten the Sunni Muslim-dominated regime in Baghdad.

The Iraqis have no illusions about Iran's intention. In a speech in Tehran in 1984 the speaker of the Iranian parliament, Ali Hashemi Rafsanjani, spelt it out clearly:

'The thing that no-one should conceal or have the intention of hiding is the export of Islamic revolution. The Islamic revolution does not confine its true and noble nature to geographical borders and deems the conveying of the message of revolution, which is the self-same message of Islam, as its own duty . . .'

At the time the war started, the general assessment outside Iran was that things were not going well for the country after the first flush of jubilation which followed the overthrow of the Shah. The armed forces were in disarray, the economy in difficulties. On the face of it, a quick military operation on the part of Iraq might have seemed tempting. What the world did not bargain for was the ardour with which the Iranians were prepared to do battle and the willingness with which they were prepared to give their lives for their religion and their country. For Shiite Muslims, to lose your life fighting a *jihad* (holy war) is considered an honour and a sure path to paradise. What Iran lacked in weapons it made up for in manpower and faith.

The Shah had made Iran into a formidable military power by acquiring the latest armaments and technology from the United

States. After the revolution, though, many of the best trained men in the forces left, and the supply of spare parts for the US-made equipment dried up. In terms of equipment, Iraq's arsenal greatly outweighs that of Iran. In 1985, for example, military experts in the Gulf estimated that the Iranian Air Force had only about 120 aircraft, of which no more than 70 or 80 were airworthy. Against this, Iraq's air wing contained some 600 combat planes. There are similar stark differences in the quantities of tanks and other heavy armour possessed by the two sides.

On a day-to-day basis, the pattern of the war has varied considerably, with long periods with little activity at all. In the early days it was mostly a land war, despite a few air raids on each other's capitals. Once the Iranian troops had blocked the initial Iraqi thrust, the Iranians soon felt confident enough to launch counter attacks. By the spring of 1982, the Iranians were back in the city of Khoramshahr, which had fallen in the early days of the war; before the year was out they had moved across parts of the Iraqi border.

At such times of heavy fighting each country issues strings of military communiqués, detailing what operation has been carried out, where, and with what result. Inevitably each side claims heavy (and without question very exaggerated) enemy losses. It's often said that if the losses claimed in the war communiqués had been accurate, then the war would be over because each country would have run out of people to fight. During quieter periods sometimes only one communiqué a day will be issued, and while the action might be limited there is never any shortage of detail, as this example from 31 October 1984 shows:

'Communiqué No. 1636. An enemy patrol was driven back and 62 rifles, 20 light rocket launchers and 7 machine-guns were captured. There was firing on enemy positions in the northern sector killing 7; firing in the sectors each of Basra and Misan; and an unsuccessful enemy air raid on the ports of Bakr and Amiq – the planes were intercepted and forced to flee by Iraqi air defences.'

Since becoming bogged down in the war Iraq has been trying to find a way of ending it, stating time and again its willingness to accept mediation. Numerous mediation teams have been formed, at various times by the United Nations, the Islamic Congress, and other organisations, and by individual countries inside and outside the region. These have come to nothing because Iran has refused to agree to mediation. The Iranians say there can be no end to the war until President Saddam Hussein is removed from power and Iraq agrees to pay millions of pounds reparation for war damage. Not surprisingly, Baghdad regards these terms as unacceptable pre-conditions for beginning talks. For a time the United Nations secured an agreement from both sides not to hit civilian targets – but it was short-lived. Iran has said it is prepared to agree to another limited truce of this kind; however, Iraq says it is interested only in an overall settlement of the conflict.

So, to try to force the Iranians into agreeing to an end to the war, the Iraqis, frustrated by their failure to defeat Iran on the battlefield, had to think of other ways of applying pressure. They did this by creating a new pattern in the war by declaring a military exclusion zone in the northern waters of the Gulf, waters which include the site of Iran's main oil terminal at Kharg Island. From the end of 1982 Iraqi planes began attacking ships using this terminal to try to halt Iranian oil exports. The attacks have, on the whole, been sporadic and have not had the desired effect, although some foreign ships stopped coming to Kharg, partly because of the danger, but mostly because of the ensuing rise in insurance rates. Also the attacks prompted Iranian reprisal raids on Arab-owned ships and vessels using Arab oil terminals.

In 1985, the Iraqis launched hundreds of raids on Kharg Island itself, but still failed to stop the export of Iranian oil, the Iranians using ships to shuttle the oil to makeshift export terminals further down the Gulf further from the Iraqi air-bases, where the crude is transferred to foreign vessels. By the end of 1986 oil industry sources in the Gulf were suggesting that all the berths at Kharg were unusable – the only outlet being a pipeline linking tankers with the shore terminal.

The Iranians, for their part, have threatened to block the straits of Hormuz at the entrance to the Gulf 500 miles further south if their oil installations are destroyed. One sixth of the oil consumed by the Western world passes through this narrow channel, so the threat was taken seriously by the oil producers and their customers. And if it were to be carried out it might bring the United States into the conflict, with a possible super-power clash. These days the feeling is that just as Iraq will probably never cut off Iran's oil exports, so Iran will never be able to block the Gulf. The land on the southern side of the Straits of Hormuz belongs to Oman, and a senior military officer there discounted the Iranian threat. To block the passage, he said, Iran would have to sink five supertankers, one upon the other.

If it is true that the Gulf war has become the forgotten conflict, then it must be in part because it has been a frustratingly difficult war to report. Apart from a short period at the start the two countries have been reluctant to allow reporters near the front lines except occasionally after a major battle when they are taken to specific spots to be shown evidence of how the particular victory was achieved. And from the Iraqi side, at any rate, it is very difficult to get an idea of the scale of the human suffering. For Iraq is a country obsessed with secrecy; there are no official figures issued about anything, not even trade or the gross national product, let alone such a sensitive matter as war casualties. So it's a matter of speculation just how many hundreds of thousands of Iraqis have been killed or injured. But there can scarcely be a family that cannot count a casualty among its relatives.

You do get occasional glimpses of the human angle under the overwhelming military blanket with which the war has forced Iraq to cover itself. On the way from Basra to Baghdad, threading our way through the seemingly endless convoys of tank transporters and countless other military vehicles, I saw a soldier by the roadside with his wife and two children. For one instant I could imagine the last choking moments he was spending with his family – moments familiar to every soldier in war time.

That trip to Basra was arranged by the Iraqis to show that the main highway from the capital was now open again and safe. A week or two earlier the Iranians had launched a massive attack across the Huwaiza marshes; wave after wave of soldiers, lightly armed and with no natural cover and no air cover had set off in small boats across the marshes, terrain where artillery can't be used, and had reached dry ground, penetrating the Iraqi defences. Eventually the superior Iraqi armour and air power forced the invaders back. It was a chilling example, though, of how Iran is prepared to sacrifice thousands upon thousands of its much larger, though hopelessly ill-equipped population (estimated at around forty-two million); or perhaps, more accurately, of how so many Iranians were prepared to take part in an attack which military experts say was bound to end in huge loss of life for Iran, even if they had succeeded in holding the territory they won. In the event it's reckoned that in this one offensive alone the Iranians lost up to 30 000 of their men, while Iraqi losses were estimated at about

10 000. On this occasion, as in previous battles, the Iranians accused Iraq of using chemical weapons, and a UN team has established that such weapons have indeed been used in the war.

The official media in Iraq proclaimed the repulsion of the Iranian attack as a famous and historic victory; banners and posters were put up around Baghdad saying as much, and Iraqi television broadcast long sequences of film showing Iranian corpses on the battlefield. There was no mention of losses, nor of the unexpectedly tough Iranian push and how close it had come to succeeding.

Ordinary Iraqis have no platform on which to express their feelings about the war one way or the other. It is undoubtedly true to say, though, that every one of them is tired of it. On the surface the war has not had a major effect on life in the capital, Baghdad. Arriving by air you enter a modern terminal building and sleek motorways speed you into the city centre, which is matted with flyovers and underpasses and where modern skyscrapers and luxury hotels dominate the skyline. Newly built mosques, their domes and minarets richly decorated, give splashes of turquoise to an otherwise drab city.

This is not the Baghdad of *The Arabian Nights*, nor of a warm evening in the 1940s which my mother recalls with nostalgia when she danced the tango with my father on the lawns under the waving palms at the Al-Wiyeh Club, a meeting place for expatriates close to the River Tigris. This is a modern capital, and the capital of a city at war. A sign in the hotel room will tell you what to do 'in the unlikely event of an unfriendly aircraft penetrating Iraqi airspace.' Only occasionally has the war come to the city itself. In March 1985 while staying in Baghdad I witnessed a series of Iranian missile attacks. One missile landed in a riverside garden close to my hotel in the city centre, smashing the windows in all the surrounding buildings. Security men stopped me approaching the gardens saying there had been 'a traffic accident'. The next morning people went to work as though nothing had happened. Such attacks were very sporadic and very brief because, it was assumed, Iran did not possess many rockets, and what it had were no match for the latest Russian models that Iraq had been firing into Iranian towns and cities. The latter months of 1986 saw further missile attacks on Baghdad.

In the face of these difficulties and the continuing frustration at being unable to end the war, President Saddam Hussein has been portraying the conflict to his people as a battle to defend Arab and Islamic values against 'Persian' aggression. There are frequent references to the Arab victories over the Persians in the seventh century and the President encourages comparisons of this kind. At a hospital in Basra I saw a poster showing President Hussein superimposed on a background of what looked like a mediaeval battlefield. The slogan referred to 'the days of the glorious knights' and praised the President for reviving the glory of the Arabs.

President Saddam Hussein portrays the war as a crusade being fought by Iraq on behalf of the Arab world as a whole to keep at bay the Shiite fundamentalists of Iran. So he expects the Arabs to provide support for his crusade. The Gulf states, led by Saudi Arabia, have provided finance, the Egyptians have given equipment, and the Jordanians have given the Iraqis access to the sea by allowing supplies to be offloaded at Aqaba on the Red Sea and transported overland through Jordan to Iraq. A steady stream of lorries chokes the long road across the desert.

Iraq is also in a unique position in the region, enjoying the support of both super-powers. The Soviet Union has long been a friend of Iraq, supplying most of its military equipment. But in recent years the government in Baghdad has taken a more pragmatic view of life, moderating some of its previously held views and seeking renewed ties with the West. Relations were re-established with the United States, and the Americans now supply the Iraqi war machine, this once again putting Iraq in a potentially much stronger position than Iran, which has no major outside backing.

The Iraqis now believe they have proved that while they may not be able to win the war they are in no danger of losing it either. What they want is peace so that they can exploit their natural resources. Their oil reserves are second in the region only to Saudi Arabia, but with the Shatt al-Arab waterway closed they have no sea terminal for exporting it. One pipe takes oil overland to Turkey, another is being built, and a third one will take oil to Saudi Arabia for export. The Iraqis realise that if they could bring the fighting to an end, then the economic boom which was stunted by that war could get going again. Foreign economic experts agree that the long-term economic prospects for Iraq are good.

Perhaps the saddest commentary on this appalling war is that neither the Soviet Union nor the United States, or many other countries, feel inclined to help one side or the other to a degree that there would be a winner or a loser. Certainly neither super-power could countenance an Iranian triumph. As long as Iran sticks to its current negotiating position, the bloody slogging match will continue in the land that is known as the cradle of civilisation.

9 The Maghreb

Lands of the west

The Air Algérie Boeing 727 on its special flight from Tehran touched down at Algiers airport in the early hours of a rain-sodden January morning in 1981. By means of a telephone installed especially on the edge of the tarmac I was reporting the arrival 'live' into a late-night radio programme in London. The people in London in fact had a better view than I did of what was happening, because they were watching close-up pictures live on television. So was most of the United States. For on board the plane, and soon to walk smiling and dazed down the aircraft steps, were the fifty-three American hostages who had been held in the US Embassy in post-Islamic revolution Tehran since November 1979. Algeria had acted as mediator and had won international acclaim for the patient and skilful way in which it had performed this role.

Algeria had been in a particularly good position to be the mediator. It was an Arab, African and Islamic state with revolutionary credentials, having fought the French for independence and subsequently having adopted a socialist system and having become a leading member of the non-aligned movement. On the other hand, its long experience under French rule, and its proximity to and close ties with Europe, gave it an understanding of the Western way of thinking. Algeria, in short, had a foot in both camps and was trusted by both.

These are the mixtures you find common to the three Maghreb countries, Algeria, Morocco and Tunisia: racially, the majority of the people are not Arabs but Berbers – the indigenous peoples of North Africa scattered widely in tribes from the Atlantic coast eastwards into Libya and even as far as Egypt. The Berbers were Arabised over the years following the birth of Islam and the Arab expansion in the seventh and eighth centuries but still kept something of the African character. Nevertheless, nowadays they are overwhelmingly Arab in outlook; all the countries share a Mediterranean shoreline, all have had colonial experiences with the French and all look to Europe for their main trade links. Indeed many migrant workers from Maghreb countries moved to Europe to find

work in Spain and, above all, France. 'This is the crossing point,' a
Moroccan minister told me of his country 'where continents and
civilisations meet.' A distinguished former diplomat in Tunis said:
'We in Tunisia like to feel we are a cross-roads; we are the joker in
the pack, with a role to play wherever we are placed.' And the view
of an Algerian government official: 'We are a bridge between the
Arabs and the Africans on one side, and Europe on the other.'

Very similar visions. In many ways each individual country
differs from the other two, but travelling through the three you can
sense some common threads, some common feelings. Certainly
the atmosphere, the scenery and the climate all feel very different
from the rest of the Arab world. One of the most distinguished historians in the Maghreb ('the west' – the grouping of the three most
westerly Arab countries) is Professor Abadallah Laroui of Rabat
University in Morocco. He sees the distinction like this: 'There's a
line between the Maghreb and the Mashreq ('the east' – the
easterly Arab countries) somewhere around Tripoli in Libya. Once
you cross that line, you no longer feel you are in the Maghreb. Even
the vernacular Arabic is different.' Lakhdar Brahimi, former
Algerian Ambassador to London agrees: 'The Libyan and Algerian
deserts are natural barriers between the two wings of the Arab
world. Then there's the Berber element which runs through the

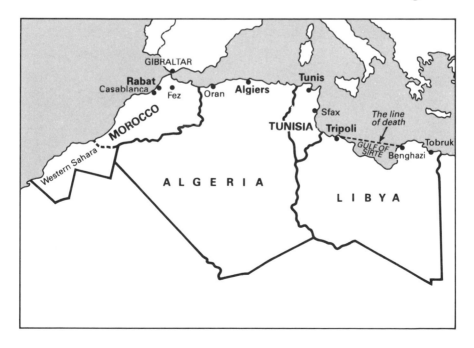

Maghreb people, setting them apart from the other Arabs.'

Given this 'distinct flavour of the Maghreb' (as one Tunisian described it to me), it is perhaps a surprise that there is not a greater amount of co-operation and co-ordination among the three countries. Maghreb unity is a theme talked about throughout the area. Many people I spoke to suggested that the first step towards unity would be in matters of trade and economic co-operation. The Maghreb might form an economic community along the lines of the one in Europe, thus expanding both the combined workforce and the combined markets for the products and produce. But so far, with the three countries competing very often for the same kind of markets, this remains only an idea.

'The people of the Maghreb believe in, and long for, greater co-operation, closer relations and maybe unity,' one Algerian told me. 'But there are differences now which are slowing things down.' So often I was told how the three countries share the same blood, same religion, and same culture. 'Our constitution says Tunisia is part of the Maghreb and that we will work for its unity. We're trying to understand why it hasn't happened.' One current 'difference', one immediate obstacle is the western Sahara dispute.

This dispute, which has soured relations between the Maghreb countries, is centred on a former Spanish colony situated to the south west of Morocco. By the mid-1970s, Spain was indicating its intention of giving up the territories called 'Spanish Sahara'. At the beginning of November 1975 King Hassan II of Morocco organised one of the most extraordinary events ever witnessed in the region – the so-called 'Green March'. An estimated 350 000 unarmed civilians walked across the border into Spanish Sahara to demonstrate Morocco's claim to sovereignty. The marchers made little progress beyond the border before being turned back by the Spanish. But King Hassan was satisfied. Later that month Spain agreed to cede its colony to the two neighbouring countries, Morocco taking over the northern areas, and Mauritania the south. This arrangement, however, did not please those sections of the indigenous population who had (and continue to have today) aspirations of independence. A liberation movement called by the acronym Polisario was formed to fight for independence. Both Morocco and Mauritania were forced to spend large amounts of money fighting the guerrillas in some of the most sandy and inhospitable terrain in Africa. In 1976 the Polisario proclaimed (from exile) the independence of the Saharan Arab Democratic Republic.

Three years later, Mauritania pulled its forces out of the territory, leaving Morocco to take over the whole area. Since then, fighting between Moroccan forces and Polisario guerrillas has continued. But it has become less intense in recent years because Morocco has built a 120-mile long defence wall from a point-east of the Atlas mountains to the coast. The 'wall of sand' as it is known, armed and manned at regular intervals along its huge length, has largely succeeded in controlling Polisario activities.

So much for the background. What is crucial about the dispute in the context of Maghreb unity is that Algeria backs Polisario, that the guerrillas operate from Algerian territory with Algerian backing, and that the leaders of the Saharan Arab Democratic Republic are based in Algiers. The newly proclaimed republic is recognised by sixty-four countries and is a member of the Organisation of African Unity, a fact which has prompted Morocco to pull out of this alliance.

Morocco
Morocco is different from any other Arab country, so much so that at times you wonder if you are in the Arab world at all. Stand on the beach near Rabat and watch the Atlantic rollers smashing onto the rocks and you feel you could be in Cornwall or Brittany; walk inland up the Bou Regreg river which flows languidly to the sea with a background of green hills and forests and you might be in Portugal; pass through one of the entrances of the medina, the old city with its orange-pink ramparts, which are beginning to crumble with age, get lost in the maze of narrow alley-ways and get drunk with the sights and evocative smells of the markets and you are firmly in the Arab world. But just as you feel reassured and you have at last discovered that, yes, appearances have been deceptive and that this really is an Arab country, you will pass a stall where there's a radio blaring out a Berber song, with its distinctive and unmistakably African beat. The sights, the faces and the atmosphere constantly change, constantly catch you off balance. The points of reference which make you feel more or less comfortable elsewhere in the Arab world tease the visitor to Morocco.

All the Maghreb countries claim to be meeting places of cultures and continents; nowhere is this more noticeable, though, than in Morocco. What's hard to fathom at first sight, too, is how the country holds together. Here you have twenty-three million people (the second largest population in the Arab world after

Egypt) with greatly varying backgrounds, with four dialects of Berber spoken, and with very considerable poverty. It seems like the classic recipe for disaster. And yet Morocco seems the calmest, most relaxed and most self-assured country in the region. You seldom see a policeman, security in public buildings is minimal. The answer seems to be that Morocco has the self-confidence of a country that has had a long, solid history. Many Moroccans use the image of an island to explain their particular characteristics. As a country it has for centuries been isolated by the Atlantic Ocean to the west, by the mountains to the east and by the Sahara desert to the south. And for much of its history it has been a cohesive unit. Even during forty-four years (1912–56) of French colonial administration (with two pockets of Spanish territory), Morocco never lost its independence. As Professor Laroui told me: 'We have for many, many centuries been a state. It was weak, that's why it was colonised by the French. But still we had a state, recognised by everyone.' Moroccans say too that the cohesiveness is maintained by two main factors: religion and the monarchy. In fact the two overlap for, as the Queen of England is Head of the Church, King Hassan, by virtue of being the thirty-fifth descendant in straight lineage of the Prophet Muhammad, is 'Amir el-Mu'mineen' literally translated as 'Prince of the Faithful', in fact signifying the position of spiritual leader of the community. Morocco is overwhelmingly Sunni Muslim, as it has been since the Arabs arrived in the seventh century. And while more than half the country speak one of the four Berber dialects (Berber is an unwritten language) as a first language, Islam and allegiance to the monarchy are common to them all. Moroccan Jews have for the most part emigrated to Israel, but some 10 000 to 15 000 remain (there is one Jewish member of parliament) and one of the daily papers continues to print the date by the Jewish calendar, along with those of the Muslim and Christian years. King Hassan has also been encouraging Moroccan Jews to return from Israel if they so wish.

Morocco may be a cross-roads of a kind today, but it was a most important one in the eighth century when the Arab armies crossed the eight miles of sea which separate the northern tip of the African continent from the southern tip of Europe. The name of the Arab commander has passed into daily use as his name was given to the distinctive rock which the Arabs saw as they approached the coast: Jebel (hill) Tariq, or, as we write it now, Gibraltar. And even today the architecture of southern Spain contains many echoes of Morocco.

But there are also fine examples of living history in Morocco itself – the mediaeval walled cities (or medinas). The biggest and finest example is Fez. Fez, incidentally, has the world's oldest university situated in the Qarawiyin mosque. Founded in 859 it predates al-Azhar University in Cairo and the first European universities by more than a century. Today no fewer than half a million people eat, sleep and work in the medina of Fez, which drops down from a plateau into the embrace of the surrounding green hills. To step inside is to step back centuries. Jostled by the donkeys (the only form of transport), with their owners shouting *Balek! Balek!* 'Mind your backs!', here you will see the men beating copper as they shape the huge vats which are used for cooking *couscous* (semolina, served with meat, fish or vegetable stew), another man melting and moulding cow horns to make combs and shoe horns, old men with their glasses, sitting cross legged, picking patiently with needles as they weave the thin threads for the tassles on the traditional cloaks which are still widely worn. And much much more. All carrying on work that has been done in the same cramped conditions and in the same style for centuries. One old man, working on the copper, said his family had been in the same business for hundreds of years. Times were harder now because aluminium was gradually winning the market. But he could not contemplate living anywhere else.

The Moroccans are well aware, though, that dwelling on the past will not help them overcome their very considerable economic problems. Morocco is a major aid recipient and, unlike its North African neighbours, does not have an oil industry. The past five years have been particularly difficult. When I visited Morocco at the beginning of 1986, there was torrential rain every day. The Moroccans were delighted. For it followed five years during which there had been a chronic shortage of rain. In a country where sixty per cent of the population live off the land, rain is vital. 'What you are seeing is not just rain, it's two billion dollars,' was one comment. During the lean years Morocco, normally self-sufficient in wheat, had to import it. As I was told by Ali Bahaijoub of the Maghreb Press Agency: 'Wheat is essential because the Moroccans can't eat without bread. Wheat for the Moroccans is like rice for the Chinese.'

The past years have also been difficult because of rising oil prices and a drop in the price of phosphates, one of the country's major exports. However, with signs of falling oil prices and good rains, the economic prospects are now brighter.

Another key concern for Morocco and all the Maghreb states is the entry of Spain and Portugal into the European Economic Community (EEC), as both those countries produce the kind of foods, like citrus fruit and olive oil, that are exported from North Africa. Morocco has decided that part of the answer is to join the EEC, and has applied to do so. Mr Azzedin Guessous is the minister with the job of cultivating Morocco's links with the community. As we chatted, we drank the sweet mint tea which is taken in large quantities throughout the country – a habit said to have been acquired from the British in the last century. Mr Guessous argues that Morocco would be a natural extension of the community. Morocco is situated closer to the heart of Europe than, for example, Greece. The problem of language is no more than it might be for, say, Portugal or Greece, for French is widely spoken in Morocco and English is growing in popularity. And while Morocco would be the only Islamic country of the EEC, in the minister's words 'Islam in Morocco is very open-minded.'

The other reason Mr Guessous cites for Morocco's application is the desire to consolidate democracy by joining a bloc of democratic states like the EEC. However, Moroccans are realistic: they realise that even if their application is successful, it will be a long process. As Professor Laroui said: 'There are huge differences, political, geographical, moral and sociological. It's difficult for a European of any political persuasion to think of North Africa as part of Europe.' But he went on to point out that thirty or forty years ago many Europeans did not consider Spain and Portugal as part of Europe either.

In looking to Europe, Morocco is not turning its back on the Arab and African worlds. It's a country that is used to variety and wants quietly to find the best way forward. In the last century Britain had close ties with Morocco. It used to import Moroccan wheat through Manchester where a small Moroccan community grew up. In the sumptuous library in the Royal Palace in Rabat I saw an economic and maritime treaty signed between Britain and Morocco in the last century. It bears the signature of a British Plenipotentiary Minister, Sir John Hay Drummond Hay [sic] and is endorsed by Queen Victoria. That treaty is still valid today. Morocco is full of surprises.

As if to underline his country's assertion that it is different from other states in the region King Hassan has never made a secret of his links with Israel. As I have said, the Jewish community in Morocco enjoys an unfettered life. Israeli representatives have attended openly Jewish congresses in Morocco. But no-one was ready for the surprise which the King was to throw in July 1986. To the astonishment of the world the Israeli Prime Minister of the day, Mr Shimon Peres, flew to Morocco for talks. Part of the Arab world was shocked, part enraged. Syria immediately broke off diplomatic relations. The talks, in fact, got nowhere; and in the end they harmed Morocco's standing in the Arab world more than they enhanced it. The King apparently recognised as much. He said the talks were meant only to be an exchange of views, adding that he'd brought them to a halt when Mr Peres said he would never negotiate with the PLO. But the damage had been done. King Hassan announced his country's resignation as Chairman of the Arab summit.

Algeria

By contrast with the soft tones of life in Morocco, albeit embroidered with chronic rural poverty, Algeria seems stern and severe. The atmosphere seems less relaxed, the society much more tightly controlled. The long, bloody war of independence left a scar which still has not been erased. And it's scarcely any wonder. For that war left more than one million people dead. All three Maghreb countries were victims of French colonial ambitions, but in Algeria the French went much further, incorporating the country into France. Algeria was simply one more *département* of France.

The French began acquiring land and property in Algeria in 1830, and in 1871 it was declared a *département*, with the French settlers establishing themselves as the power of the land. By the 1930s and 1940s, the discontent of the Arab and Berber populations was beginning to show itself in public demonstrations which were broken up with ruthless force by the European settlers. In riots in 1945, for example, it is estimated that 15 000 Muslims were killed. The hatred was born. Much worse was to come. Two years later, under a new constitution, everyone living in Algeria was given French citizenship and French voting rights. But the Muslims were set on achieving nothing less than independence. The 1950s saw the violence increased and saw the formation of organised political and military resistance to the European settlers, the Front de Libération Nationale (FLN) leading the former and the Armée de

Libération Nationale (ALN) the latter. ALN carried out a series of bomb attacks and other acts of violence directed at European targets, each time drawing savage French retaliation. Eventually the settlers themselves struck back, forming their own defence committees and demanding the full integration of Algeria into France. Later the Organisation de l'Armée Secrète (OAS) was established, in response to a French decision to negotiate with the FLN and a growing realisation that France was beginning to suggest that the Algerians had the right to decide their own fate. The OAS went on the rampage, killing Muslims at random. They even tried to take control of the capital. But while they wrought havoc (there was even a bombing campaign in Paris) they could not stem the inevitable tide which was pulling Algeria towards independence. In March 1962, France promised Algeria independence after a transition period and in July that year it was proclaimed. The OAS had lost the struggle, but they had gone down flailing at everything, and thousands more Muslims were killed.

And once independence had been won, the settlers packed their bags and left. Some one million of them from all walks of life, but especially from the professional, skilled worker and managerial classes, abandoned their homes and abandoned Algeria, most of them going back to France. These were the famous *pieds noirs*. The cost of freedom to Algeria, then, was doubly appalling.

The man who first had the job of trying to put this crippled country on its feet again was Ahmed Ben Bella, who had played a leading part in the early days of the struggle for independence. He had to flee the country in 1949. He was back in 1957, although not in circumstances that he would have chosen. A French pilot flying him and other FLN notables from Morocco to Tunisia landed his plane in Algiers. Ben Bella was arrested and held in France. In September 1963 he was not only back in his homeland, but was being acclaimed as Algeria's first president. He had formidable problems to cope with, not least among his own colleagues who disputed not only who should lead Algeria, but also how it should be run. Ben Bella's answer was to draw more and more power into his own grasp. This was one of the causes of dissatisfaction which led to the military coup of June 1965. Ben Bella was arrested, remaining in detention until 1980 when he went once more into exile. Five years later he was in London announcing the formation of a new Algerian opposition group.

The new president was the defence minister, Houari Boumedienne. The subsequent years saw Algeria at the forefront of the radical world – it gained a reputation of being a country which was fiercely anti-West, fiercely anti-Israeli and strongly supportive of those Arab countries which rejected a peace settlement with Israel. It was regarded too as a safe haven for hijackers.

Since President Boumedienne's death in 1978, the new leader, President Chadli Benjedid, has done much to soften Algeria's image, so that Algeria today condemns hijacking, for example, with as much vigour as any other country. It also has a much more flexible foreign policy, seeking better relations with the West (in 1985 President Chadli became the first Algerian president to visit the United States) while keeping on good terms with socialist and revolutionary states, in addition to playing a leading and very respected role in the Movement of Non-Aligned Nations (hence Algeria's ability to act as go-between in the affairs of the US hostages in Tehran). Algeria remains a socialist, one-party state. But President Chadli has encouraged the role of the private sector in industry and agriculture. This sector played a minimal role under President Boumedienne, and the cumbersome state machinery often proved inflexible and inadequate to cope with the needs of farmers and industrialists, leading to frequent shortages in the shops.

Some of the other changes have been in response to domestic problems. For example, the Islamic character of Algeria is given much greater prominence these days than in the past. The Algerian government is aware that it has to appease Muslim fundamentalists who are fiercely critical of the secularisation of the country. In 1985, Muslim fundamentalists attacked a police training school and stole weapons from it. They've also been trying to organise a guerrilla campaign in country areas.

Algeria also faces a problem with its Berber community which believes that the government has been attempting to suppress the language. Some concessions have been made to the Berbers, but as in the other North African countries, the government is wary of giving too much emphasis to the Berber culture for fear that it could divide the nation.

Many of Algeria's problems can be traced back to the years of French domination. For while, after independence, the Algerians were anxious to rid their country of French influence, most found it impossible to do so. And ever since there has been this continuing inner conflict: the natural linguistic, cultural and commercial pull to French versus the deeply felt and publicly encouraged desire to Arabise the country. You can even see the conflict in the look of the capital with its uneasy mixture of building. Some could easily have been lifted out of southern France with their frontages decorated with wooden shutters and wrought-iron railed balconies; others are in the grand but austere and impersonal style favoured by so many third-world socialist countries, and found throughout the Arab world.

Not all problems, though, can be blamed on France. Algeria's main source of income is oil, and the country has suffered in the same way as most other producers with the slump in prices. The benefit that oil income over the years has brought to city life has resulted in many people leaving the countryside, causing (as in other North African cities) major overcrowding. And the government has the job of both finding housing and trying to encourage a return to the land. For while one may think of Algeria as a desert country, the coastal strip contains rich farmland. If you drive through this area in early spring, you could imagine yourself anywhere in northern Europe.

But desert is the main feature of this huge country (in area it is not much smaller than India), with the majority of the twenty million or so Algerians packed into Algiers and the coastal strip. The size of the country was brought home to me in 1982 when I flew in a twin-engined light aircraft from Algiers to Tamanrassat (Mark Thatcher was reported missing on a trans-Sahara car race). The journey took seven hours and still we had not reached Algeria's southern border.

Algeria has the potential to be a strong tourist attraction. But it lacks the infrastructure, and these days lacks the money to build it. And one feels, in any case, that the country would have to learn first to relax a little.

Tunisia

A statue of President Habib Bourguiba on horseback stands in a dominating position at the top of the main avenue in Tunis. It is fitting that it should, for the whole country is dominated by that one man. He founded the Neo-Destour (New Constitution) party in 1934; that same party runs Tunisia today. He led the resistance to French colonial rule, and has been President of Tunisia since independence in 1956. From a palace tucked in the woods on the coast just outside Tunis, in the shadow of the rather desultory ruins of the Roman city of Carthage, President Bourguiba has directed every aspect of Tunisia life since 1956. He's a man prone to whims and sudden changes of course that have had the effect of unsettling friends and foes alike. He's been quick to squash anyone who might challenge his supremacy. So, over past years as he's approached his mid-eighties and as his health has continued to be frail, a major talking point has been: who will succeed him and when? At times one can't help feeling that this has been a diversion from some of the more pressing issues of the day which needed more attention.

President Bourguiba has created a country which in outlook and in some places, notably the capital, is more European than any other Arab country. A good number of the street and shop signs in Tunis are written exclusively in French, and it's the kind of city where if as a foreigner you ask a question in Arabic, the answer will invariably come in French. The clothing fashions too in the capital mirror France. So for the one million or more Europeans who come as tourists each year, the culture shock is not as great as it might be in some other countries.

What's interesting, furthermore, is that the latest figures on tourism show more than two million people visiting Tunisia each year, of whom 700 000 are from Maghreb countries, almost all from neighbouring Algeria. Tunisians derive wry satisfaction from the fact that the vast majority of these visitors come over the border to buy goods that are not available in the austere shops in Algeria. Tunisia, in fact, has the image of being a relaxed, pro-Western state, keeping on the sidelines of the main controversies in the region. People who know the country well, however, know that beneath the surface things are not so calm.

To gather material for the BBC radio series *The Arab World* I returned to Tunis after a fifteen-year gap. I made a pilgrimage to the old lodging house where I'd stayed while attending a course at Tunis University. The building had been knocked down. It was just one of a number of disappointments.

In general the city, despite the appearance of more luxury hotels and other high-rise buildings, was looking decidedly down-at-heel compared with fifteen years ago. It seemed to have lost its sparkle; it is neither chic and efficient nor old-world and charming. When I raised this point I was told that it was a reflection of serious economic difficulties which the country was just beginning to face. 'Hard times are just around the corner, and I tremble to think what social and political problems will come with them,' was one assessment I heard.

The reasons for the economic troubles are not hard to find. Tunisian oil exports (the main money-winner) have been hit like everyone else's. Remittances from the tens of thousands of Tunisians working abroad are dropping because of the world recession and unemployment in Europe. The prospect for the sale of citrus fruit and olive oil has worsened now that Spain, Portugal and Greece have joined the European Economic Community; and tourism, while holding steady, is not developing.

The main problem, I was told on many occasions, is youth unemployment. Certainly the Parisian-style cafés in Tunis, once the favourite meeting-places for men and women of all ages, are patronised almost exclusively these days by men who look as though they have nothing to do. A young lady university teacher confirmed this impression. 'I used to go to cafés, but not any more. I don't feel comfortable. They're full of country people who've come to Tunis looking for work. And they stare at you in a way that makes you feel uneasy,' she said.

This change of atmosphere, this sense of unease that rising unemployment coupled with pegged salaries and rising prices can bring, taken together make many foreign diplomats in Tunis worried about the future. And the diplomats point to the riots of January 1984 as an example of what could so easily break out. The riots (one Tunisian journalist described them as a 'mini-revolution') were sparked off by an overnight doubling of the cost of bread and a cut in government subsidies on other essential goods. Scores of people were killed and hundreds wounded as crowds attacked shops and cars and other signs of consumerism. President Bourguiba had no choice but to cancel the price rises.

It is thought that the riots many have been fuelled by Muslim fundamentalists, members of the banned Mouvement de la Tendance Islamique (MTI). While the number of its supporters is not known, many Tunisians I spoke to believe that this is a significant force and could grow in popularity if living and working conditions worsened.

One of the aims of MTI is to destroy all the reforms of the 1960s, which made Tunisia today, in the words of one Tunisian journalist 'much more secular than any other Arab Islamic country'. These reforms included changes in the legal status of women which were among the most progressive in the Arab world. In their dress and social behaviour, Tunisian women seem much freer than any others; but they are quick to point out that while this may be so in the capital, it is not the case in the rural areas, where you still find a high percentage of the women, young and old, wearing the traditional veil. A university lecturer in Tunis told me how she had attended a Saharan festival in the south of the country. Government posters in the towns and villages there urged women to come forward and play a role in society. But the local women ignored them completely. And they stared at the university lecturer in her European clothes as they would have done at a foreigner. This distinction between town and country should not be underestimated in any Arab country; but it's perhaps particularly true in Tunisia, where people complain about the lack of social and recreational facilities outside the two main population centres (Tunis and Sfax).

This new mood in Tunisia has made the question of the succession more important than ever. By the beginning of 1986, with the President's son, Habib Bourguiba Junior, having fallen out of favour, it looked as though the job would go to the Prime Minister, Mohamed Mzali. Most worrying to foreign observers was the way in which Mr Mzali appeared to be preparing the country for the traumatic day when the Tunisians lost the only father-figure they've known. Instead of trying to win support and build confidence, he purged the main platform for opposition in Tunisia, the trade union movement. Not for the first time in his life, the veteran trade union leader Habib Achour (thought of by some as a potential candidate for president) found himself in prison, and all his supporters were removed from senior posts, to be replaced by 'party' men. And to underline the sense of insecurity surrounding the question of the succession, by the end of 1986 Mr Mzali himself had been dismissed; what's more, he had a good idea of the sort of fate that can befall Tunisian Prime Ministers who drop out of favour, and so he fled the country.

There has been a great deal of talk in Tunisia about what 'might' happen. Equally many of the gloomy predictions may turn out to be wrong. The government may be able to ride the economic storm in such a way that there will be no repeat of the 'mini-revolution'. And in the meantime, Tunisia continues to be an important point of contact between the Arab world and the West, and for millions of Europeans, Tunisia will be their only experience of the Arab or Islamic worlds. (The mosque at Kairouan, once the western capital of the Arab empire, is one of the most impressive that I've seen.) Some orientalists say that Tunisia, with its modern looks and liberal outlook, is untypical of the Arab world, therefore giving a false impression. This is nonsense. Every Arab country is different from every other. The word 'typical' in this context is meaningless.

In any event, since Egypt was expelled from the Arab League because of the peace treaties signed with Israel by President Sadat, Tunis has been the home of the Arab League headquarters. It was to Tunis that the PLO Chairman, Mr Yasir Arafat, moved his headquarters in 1982 after being pushed out of Lebanon by the Israelis. It is precisely because Tunisia has stayed as much as possible out of regional conflicts that it is an obvious base for such organisations. Nothing would suit Tunisia better than to be able to maintain this policy of live and let live, at home and abroad.

Libya

President Reagan has called him 'that madman of the Mediterranean'. Anwar Sadat, the former President of Egypt, used the same description. Many other world leaders have no doubt expressed similar sentiments in private. Colonel Muammar Qadafi: in the minds of most people in the world his name is synonymous with the country which he has led since 1969 – Libya, a huge wedge of North African desert which dips a thousand miles down into the Sahara and is crowned by a thin strip of fertile coastline. In that strip are situated the two cities of Tripoli (to the northwest of the country) and Benghazi (to the northeast) where most of Libya's three and a half million inhabitants live.

Colonel Qadafi has been, to put it mildly, an unusual and idiosyncratic leader. His style of leadership, his political philosophy and his personal charisma have drawn worldwide attention to Libya which far exceeds the size of its population, its economic strength or strategic usefulness. The prominence which President Reagan accorded Libya in the first half of 1986 is the best example of a widespread distorted vision of the country.

Libya, like its Maghreb neighbours to the west, was a victim of colonial designs and, furthermore, provided the stage for some of the fiercest battles in the Second World War. While the French were the colonial masters in the west, Italy was the European power which began occupying Libya in the mid-1920s, developing the rich farmland in the northern strip, planting trees to protect the soil from the winds which blew in the sands from the Sahara and building roads to bring the produce to the cities for export. Many Italian families settled in Libya, and remnants of Italian architecture can still be seen in both the cities and the countryside.

The Second World War saw the Allied Armies driving the Italians out of Libya, making Tripoli, Benghazi, Tobruk and other places household names in Britain. With Britain and France eventually occupying different areas of the country, it was the United Nations which finally decided that Libya should become independent. This it did at the end of 1951. But it was an independence with limitations. Both Britain and the United States negotiated the right to maintain military bases in the country and these were still in place in the late 1960s when I went as a student to stay with my sister who was at that time working in Tripoli. I remember – amid the picnics along the hundreds of miles of untouched Mediterranean coastline and amid the sightseeing tours to the incredibly well preserved Roman ruins at Leptis Magna – parties at the Wheelus US Air Force base just outside the capital. But things were about to change. Even then, there were some towns and villages where cars carrying Europeans were liable to be pelted with stones. Colonial memories are not easily erased.

The change itself came in September 1969 when a group of young army officers took the opportunity of a visit by the reigning monarch, King Idris, to Turkey for medical treatment to stage a coup. The officers were led by twenty-seven year old Colonel Muammar Qadafi. At the time no-one could have foreseen how great that change was to be. All that was clear at first as the officers formed their Revolutionary Command Council was that the new regime was radical in outlook (it immediately won the backing of radical and socialist states throughout the world) and fiercely anti-Western (the West being regarded as synonymous with 'colonial' and 'imperialist').

The new policies were soon put into practice. By the time I next visited Libya in the early 1970s, the British and American bases had gone, all public signs in English (including street signs) had been removed, Arabic was the required language for foreigners' passport particulars, the sale of alcohol was banned and Islamic codes were being enforced as never before. The beauty of the sweeping corniche in Tripoli had been ruined because the sea immediately in front of it had been reclaimed and the new land filled with ships' containers. At sea, dozens of ships lay at anchor awaiting their turn to enter the congested port. But in the evening the city was dead.

There was no longer any night life to entice the bored sailors ashore.

The other most noticeable change was the appearance of countless slogans adorning public hoardings and taken from Colonel Qadafi's 'Green Books' in which he expounds his thoughts about a new order for society based on a mixture of socialism and Islam. And alongside these slogans were pictures of the Colonel himself, many of them side by side with photos of former President Nasser of Egypt, the champion of the cause of pan-Arab unity. For Colonel Qadafi believes that he is Nasser's successor and the only true guardian of the principle of pan-Arabism. His years as leader have been characterised by numerous plans to unite Libya with other Arab states. At various times and with great acclaim plans have been announced for unions with Egypt, Sudan, Syria, Tunisia and, most recently, Morocco.

None of these schemes has come to fruition. Instead relations with Egypt in recent years have been strained to the extent that there have been border incidents between the two countries. The same is true about relations with Tunisia. Like much that Colonel Qadafi has said and done, the aim of inter-Arab union was hopelessly unrealistic. The Arab world listened to the stirring words of President Nasser and others in the 1950s and early '60s. They pinned their hopes on a new secular order which would blend the Arab nations into one family. And then they saw Arab nationalism discredited on the battlefield in the war with Israel in 1967. In the 1970s, on the whole, Arab leaders listened out of politeness to what the Libyan leader was saying, but put little store by it.

Another key policy was to give financial and military support to 'liberation movements' across the world. (By the seventies oil was making Libya a rich nation. In 1971, the assets of British Petroleum had been nationalised, which angered a number of leaders both inside and outside the Arab world.) Sudan on a number of occasions accused Libya of being behind coup attempts inside their territory. Egypt saw Libyan complicity in acts of sabotage in Cairo and elsewhere and Morocco was enraged by the support that the Tripoli regime gave to the Polisario (see p. 127). Indeed, the explanation given for the very surprising announcement in 1984 that Libya and Morocco were to unite was that it might lead to Tripoli dropping its support for the Polisario fighters.

While Colonel Qadafi looks keenly to the Arab world for alliances, he also looks to Africa with the aim of setting up a pan-

African and Islamic state stretching from coast to coast south of Libya. His troops have fought with the rebels in Chad and they've been involved in Uganda too. However, his Africa policy has lost him as many friends in the continent as it has won him, and a move by the Organisation of African Unity in 1982 to prevent Libya from becoming Chairman was evidence of this. At home, meanwhile, he has developed his power base by buying arms from the Soviet Union and elsewhere (vast quantities of them), and by removing from power, imprisoning or executing those people considered a threat to his leadership. From a bedouin tent pitched incongruously inside a heavily fortified military camp on the edge of Tripoli, the Colonel keeps an ear and an eye on all around him.

Libya has seen many internal changes since its coup, but the biggest was in 1977 when the already existing system of collective decision-making through People's Committees was taken to its extreme. The name 'Libya' was changed to 'The Socialist People's Libyan Arab Jamahiriya'. 'Jamahariya' is a word coined by Colonel Qadafi meaning 'the nation of the masses'. Colonel Qadafi himself renounced the title of President. The Constitution, agreed upon by a meeting of 'the Libyan Arab People' in March 1977, promulgated, among other things, that the Koran would be the social code, that 'the direct People's Authority is the basis for the political order. . .
The People shall practise its authority through People's Congresses, Popular Committees, Trade Unions, Vocational Syndicates and the General People's Congress.' Colonel Qadafi was appointed Secretary-General of the General People's Congress, but he later renounced that title too. To all intents, however, Colonel Qadafi appears to be as much 'President' as he has ever been.

These changes at home were followed by the take-over of Libyan embassies abroad by 'students' who thereafter ran them under the name of 'People's Bureaux'. And Libyans abroad were encouraged by the government, and (according to allegations made by a number of Western governments) given arms, money and support by diplomats in the People's Bureaux, to kill opponents of the Qadafi regime. A number of exiles in Britain and elsewhere were killed. So Libyans I knew in London at the time, even many who were not active opponents of the Colonel, went into hiding, and night-spots that had been favourites of the Libyan community in London were suddenly deserted.

This was the moment when the attention of the world began to turn fully onto Libya and its association with acts of violence carried out around the world and its association with terror groups in other countries (such as the Irish Republican Army and the Abu Nidal faction of the Palestinian movement). Matters began to come to a head in April 1984 when a British policewoman, Yvonne Fletcher, was killed and a number of other people were injured during an anti-Qadafi demonstration outside the People's Bureau in London. The shots had been fired from inside the Libyan building. Britain broke off diplomatic relations with Tripoli.

Over the ensuing two years, with hijacking and other acts of terror becoming commonplace in the Middle East and neighbouring Mediterranean areas, the United States began focusing on Libya as the suspected source of, or at least supporter of, much of the violence that was being directed at foreign targets in the region. The watershed appears to have been two simultaneous attacks at the airports of Rome and Vienna toward the end of 1985. Gunmen opened up on people queuing to check in for flights on the Israeli airline El Al. Many Americans were among the victims. Washington said it had evidence that Libya 'had had a hand' (it did not specify how) in these two outrages. The United States promised revenge.

So the count-down to the American raids on Libya in the first quarter of 1986 began. American diplomats in the region say Washington was determined to find a pretext to strike at Libya 'to teach Colonel Qadafi a lesson in the only language he understands'. They did this by sending the US Sixth fleet on exercises in the Mediterranean. The movements took the vessels into the Bay of Sirte off the Libyan coast. Tripoli claims the Bay as part of its territorial waters. Having already threatened that to cross 'the line of death' (as Colonel Qadafi in characteristically colourful language described it) would invite a Libyan response, the Colonel had no choice but to launch missiles at the US jets flying from the fleet. The planes in turn struck back at the missile sites.

The following weeks saw the Americans saying they had proof that Libya was behind the bombing of a night-club in West Berlin frequented by US servicemen, and that a terrorist attack on people queuing for visas at the American embassy in Paris had been averted. So, the planes went onto the offensive again, some of them taking off from aircraft carriers in the Mediterranean, others flying all the way down the western sea coast of Europe from US bases in Britain because other European countries had refused to co-operate in this American initiative.

The aim of the attack was to give the Libyans a bloody nose. But most Arab states and many countries outside the region were angered by the American response. Libya's main Arab ally, Syria, was one of the first to condemn Washington. One would not have expected less. But most other Arab countries too, both traditionally pro-Western and anti-Western alike, deplored the American action. The Gulf states, along with other pro-Western countries such as Tunisia, Egypt and Jordan, felt humiliated and embarrassed by what America had done. Colonel Qadafi may have only a handful of friends in the Arab world. His policies and his mercurial moods are as abhorrent to most Arab leaders as they are to President Reagan. But the conclusion drawn by most observers of the Middle East after the event was that the United States had made a fool of itself. Bombing Libya would not wipe out terrorism. Furthermore it would enhance the prestige of Libya and its leadership and increase the likelihood of escalating reprisals. For no Arab state can stand silently by when another country is attacked (or, as most Arabs would say, 'bullied') by a superpower. For the time being, however, Libya has expressed its anger against the two English-speaking nations involved in the attack solely by banning the teaching of English and turning its interest to the promotion of Russian.

Whatever one feels about Libya, Colonel Qadafi has managed to stay in power despite the animosity towards him inside and outside the Middle East. It is an eccentric country, fitting into none of the loose patterns which characterise other various regions in the Arab world. But it is afflicted by the same economic difficulties related to falling oil prices as any other oil-producing state. And in the end what will probably bring Libya more into line with its neighbours is not American bombs but pure necessity. Libya will not work effectively without income from oil and without a sizeable foreign workforce. The way things are going, Colonel Qadafi is in danger of losing a big percentage of both.

10 Sudan and the Yemens
At the borders of the Arab world

Twenty-one flags fly outside the modest building in Tunis housing the headquarters of the League of Arab States, but since this book is intended to be an introduction to the Arab world as a whole, rather than a comprehensive guide, not all the twenty-one states have been referred to. Specifically, because this is a personal introduction, I have omitted mention of those Arab countries which I have not visited, but nevertheless I think it would be inappropriate to close any look at the region without briefly mentioning three of the states that I have not referred to in the preceding pages: Sudan, South Yemen and North Yemen.

Sudan

As a country of nearly one million square miles (larger than Saudi Arabia) and the biggest country in the whole of Africa with a population of more than 20 million people, Sudan cannot be ignored. Like its northern neighbour Egypt, it was subject to the dubious benefits of British colonial interest in the last century, and events that occurred there and the personalities involved all contributed to impressions fostered in the West about the region as a whole. Countless British schoolboys, for example, were raised on stories about the battles to liberate Khartoum and put down the rebellion of the Mahdi ('the mad Mahdi' as I recall books saying) in the mid-1880s. The last stand leadership of General Gordon and the final defeat of the Mahdi's forces in the Battle of Omdurman are well chronicled.

These days Sudan has been hitting the headlines for other reasons: hundreds of thousands of people, possibly as many as two or even three million in the south of the country are in danger of starving to death. Food is available to be sent to them, but distribution has been blocked by a civil war which has lasted more than three years.

The origins of the war can be traced back to the policies of a man who led the country for nearly sixteen years, President Gaffar Nimeri. President Nimeri seized power with other army officers in a bloodless coup in May 1969, thirteen years after Sudan had achieved independence from Anglo-Egyptian control. In his early years in power Nimeri fostered close links with the Soviet Union and other East bloc nations. Later though, as the country's economic difficulties worsened, he turned increasingly to Egypt (then under the leadership of President Sadat) and the United States. In 1982 Sudan and Egypt signed a Charter of Integration.

A persistent theme in Sudanese history is rivalry and hostility between the north and south of the country. The north (with its capital at Khartoum where the Blue Nile and the White Nile meet) is predominantly Muslim; the south (with Juba as its capital) is populated by Christians and animists. In 1972 an agreement was signed in Addis Ababa in Ethiopia to end the civil war. However, in 1983 President Nimeri, bowing to pressure from Muslim fundamentalists, introduced the Shari'a or Islamic Law and applied it to the whole country. So it was that Christians and others in the south were subjected to traditional Islamic punishments such as the amputation of hands for theft, alcohol was banned, and so on. The people rebelled and they are still rebelling. The main group leading the rebellion is the Sudanese People's Liberation Movement (SPLM) led by a former army officer, John Garang. A key condition for ending the war is the abolition of the Shari'a.

By 1984 and 1985 growing economic problems contributed to general discontent about the leadership of President Nimeri. And nothing that he tried to do to appease the anger of the southerners or to meet demands for even tougher Islamic rules from Muslim fundamentalists in the north could erase that discontent. With the economic life of the country almost paralysed by strikes, President Nimeri went on a visit to the United States in April 1985. It was the signal for a coup led by the Minister of Defence, General Abdel-Rahman Swareddahab. The deposed President never returned and the Sudanese people rejoiced.

The expectation in the south of the country was that the new regime would abolish the Shari'a. But no change was made. In May 1986, after elections, a civilian government took over power with the Oxford-educated descendant of the Mahdi who killed General Gordon following the siege of Khartoum in 1885, Mr Sadiq el-Mahdi, becoming Prime Minister. Still no change was made, although sentences which were passed under Islamic Law were suspended. The problem that the new premier faced was continuing pressure from Islamic fundamentalists to maintain the status quo.

So the civil war continued; so did the poverty; so did the starvation. The new government began talks with SPLM and by the middle of 1986 these were said to be making good progress. In August, however, the government broke off the dialogue after the rebels in the south shot down a civilian plane, killing all sixty people on board. After that, with the plight of the starving worsening by the day, political wrangling interrupted the flow of grain and other food to the areas most in need. The rebels said the food supplies were benefiting only those areas under army control and would not give assurances of safe passage to relief planes. The government for its part was against the idea of food supplies getting to the rebels.

By the autumn of 1986 Mr Sadiq el-Mahdi was speaking of his intentions of reopening the dialogue with the SPLM. And he seemed to be determined to cut his country's overwhelming dependence on Egypt and the United States. Relations with Cairo became distinctly cooler, while those with Washington's great enemy, Libya, improved. But with the country's overseas debts rising fast and with the fierce fighting in the south of the country continuing there seems to be no easy solution to the mountain of problems facing this ailing giant of the Arab and African worlds.

South Yemen

Another Arab country fixed firmly in the minds of thousands of Britons is South Yemen – or to give it its full title, the People's Democratic Republic of Yemen. The mention of its capital, Aden, will be enough to awaken memories of the bitter anti-attack in the 1950s from fighters belonging to FLOSY (Front for the Occupation of Occupied South Yemen) and the National Liberation Front (NLF). South Yemen was most recently in the news when there was a bloody power struggle between rival Marxist and tribal groups in January 1986.

There might seem to be little of importance in this mostly desert and extremely poor country with a population of just over two million. In fact its geographical position, controlling the entrance to the Red Sea, made it a key possession of the British for nearly 140 years up to independence in 1967. Having control of Aden was essential if the sea route through the Suez Canal to India was to be secure. From 1839 onwards Aden was a regular port-of-call for British ships en route to India. It was here that they loaded up with coal or, in more modern times, oil.

In recent years the importance of the sea route linking east and west has diminished and so has the strategic importance of South Yemen. But its geographical position is such that it will always be a useful possession, and these days it provides a vital foothold for the Soviet Union on the Arabian peninsula as well as a handy base for the Russian navy in the Arabian Sea through which much of the west's oil is shipped. For since independence political and economic life in South Yemen has leaned strongly towards the Eastern bloc countries, with the Soviet Union being accorded military base facilities and Russians and East Germans providing advisers of various kinds.

The internal political system of South Yemen is also modelled on East bloc lines with a Supreme People's Council of 111 members being the highest policy-making body. This in turn elects a presidium of up to seventeen men and the chairman of the presidium becomes head of state. But woven through the fabric of South Yemeni policy is a strong thread of tribal allegiances which often transcend political considerations and obfuscate what seems obvious. So it was that the Soviet Union, with its vast embassy in Aden, seems to have been taken by surprise as much as any other state when fighting suddenly broke out in January 1986. Indeed the Russians were the first foreigners to announce the evacuation of their nationals from South Yemen. It was typical too that for the first few days after the fighting started nobody (including the Russians and the Americans) seemed to know what was going on. As the conflict continued the Russians even seemed to change their minds about which party should enjoy Soviet support. Many of the instant analyses by so-called experts on Yemeni affairs turned out to be wide of the mark.

What actually happened was a classic display of the ruthlessness of the politics of South Yemen. And the origins go back a few years to 1978 when the President of the day, Salem Rubai'a Ali, was murdered in a coup which brought Abdel-Fatah Ismail to power. He was a hardline Marxist with strong links with Moscow, and during his two years in power South Yemen became even more isolated than ever from North Yemen and its fiercely anti-communist neighbours. Ismail even signed a friendship treaty with the Soviet Union, but perhaps because Moscow wanted to try to gain influence in Saudi Arabia and the Gulf states, Ismail left the country in 1980, travelling to the Soviet Union on the grounds of ill-health. He was replaced by Ali Nasser Mohammed, a less doctrinaire Marxist than Ismail, whose pragmatic policies helped Aden improve relations with the neighbouring states. He also introduced liberal economic reforms which gained him enemies among the hard-liners. In 1985 Abdel-Fatah Ismail was allowed back from what had amounted to political exile and was given a seat on the politburo. As events turned out it is now clear that from the moment of Ismail's return Ali Nasser Mohammed felt insecure, and in line with the policy that attack is the best form of defence he ordered the murder of his political opponents as they were arriving for a meeting of the politburo. Ismail was one of those killed. In the subsequent fighting thousands of people were killed (some estimates put the figure as high as 10 000). Ali Nasser Mohammed fled to North Yemen with an estimated 6000 of his supporters, leaving a technocrat, Haider Abu Baker Attas as interim president.

For the Russians, with their embassy badly damaged in the fighting, the episode was a sobering realisation that however much Yemeni affairs may be directed from outside, the Yemenis themselves have their own way of settling old scores.

North Yemen

While Britain's colonial interests in Aden brought a measure of prosperity to South Yemen, the north of the country remained isolated and under-developed. Much of it is unchanged today. It is a land of spectacular scenery, of high volcanic plateaus and villages perched on the sides of mountains. And it is another country where traditional tribal allegiances are paramount.

The formative years for modern-day North Yemen (the Yemen Arab Republic) were 1962 to 1969 when a civil war was fought between royalists (followers of the Imam), supported by Saudi Arabia, and nationalists, backed by Egypt. At one time the Egyptians had about 50 000 troops stationed in North Yemen. The period following the end of the civil war which saw the royalists defeated was marked by sporadic fighting between government troops and followers of the Imam and by sporadic clashes across the border with South Yemen. At the same time Arab mediation continued to patch up differences between the government in the North Yemeni capital, Sana'a, and the regime in Aden. Indeed another prominent feature of this period was a succession of announcements that the two countries had sunk their differences and were working out the details of unification. The first such declaration was made in the Libyan capital, Tripoli, in October

1972; and Tripoli was again the scene of one of the most recent ones in July 1986. Yet unification has never happened and my guess is that it never will. For while South Yemen has moved unashamedly into the East bloc sphere of influence, North Yemen has followed a more ambiguous path, trying to maintain good relations with Saudi Arabia and countries of the Western bloc while at the same time buying arms and other equipment from the Soviet Union and allowing Soviet advisers to train the armed forces.

North Yemen also receives aid from both the United States and the Soviet Union and the country needs all the aid it can get. The population is estimated at around eight million, and North Yemen rates among the poorest countries in the world, a situation made worse by a major earthquake which struck the country in December 1982. Future prospects were improved, however, by the discovery of oil by an American in 1984 and the construction of a 10 000 barrel-a-day refinery.

The man who has shaped North Yemen's delicately balanced foreign policy and who has had to watch over the domestic problems is President Ali Abdullah Saleh who has been in power since 1978. He is well aware of the complexities and intrigues in political life in that southern tip of the Arabian peninsula. His predecessor was murdered by a bomb brought in a briefcase by an envoy from South Yemen. The recent fighting in South Yemen and the overthrow of the leader there who had gone out of his way to foster good relations with Sana'a will put him on his guard even more.

Of all the countries in the Arab world the two Yemens look set to remain the most difficult for the Western mind to fathom.

Index

Roman numerals refer to plates

Abdullah, King 82–3
Abu Dhabi 97, 106, iii
Abu Nidal 73, 142
Aden 149
Aflaq, Michel 91
Alawites 28, 91, 92
alcohol 30, 101, 111, 139
Aleppo 89, 90
Algeria 124, 127, 132–4;
  economy 134; French rule
  124, 131–2; independence
  131–2
Algiers 124, 127, 132, 134
Ali, Muhammed 36
Amal 61–2, 64
American University of
  Beirut 57–8
Amman 70, 80, 81, 84, 89
Anderson, Terry 57
Aqaba 88, 123
Arabic language 10, 13, 18,
  125; words used in
  English 14
Arab–Israeli war (1973) 20,
  41, 86
Arab League 20, 42, 49, 138
Arab Legion 83, 84
Arafat, Yasir: early career
  71; chairman of PLO 64,
  72; leadership of PLO 67,
  73, 76–9; withdraws PLO
  from Beirut 75–6, 138, ix;
  rejects UN resolution on
  Israel 80; relations with
  King Hussein 86, 87;
  peace negotiations with
  King Hussein 93; moves
  to Tunis 138
Armée de Libération
  Nationale (ALN) 131–2
Assad, President 73, xvi;
  accession 90, 91; domestic
  policy 92; foreign policy
  93–5
Aswan high dam 39, 40

Baath Party 8, 91
Baghdad 122, 123
Baghdad Pact 84
Bahrain 11, 97, 104, 105,
  111–13
Balfour Declaration 68–90
Basra 115–16, 121, 123, xiv

Begin, Menachim 41, 42
Beirut: civil war 45, 48–54,
  xi; Green Line 49, 51, 56,
  75; siege 50, 74–6; with-
  drawal of PLO 67, 75–6
Ben Bella, President Ahmed
  132
Benghazi 138, 139
Benjedid, President Chadli
  133
Berbers 124, 125, 128, 131,
  133
Berri, Nabih 54, 60, 64
'Black September' 72
Boumedienne, President
  Houari 132–3, xvi
Bourguiba, President Habib
  134–5

Cairo 10, 33–7, i, vi
Camp David agreements 33,
  41–2, 44
Carter, President James 33,
  41, 42, 74
Chamoun, President
  Camille 48, 62, 64
Chatila refugee camp 50,
  75–6, ix
Chouf mountains 52, 61, 62,
  66
Christian Arabs 13, 59
Christianity 23, 24
clothing 15–16, 22, 28, 101,
  109; on pilgrimage 26; in
  Tunisia 135, 136–7
Coptic Church 36
Crusades 15, 22, 90
culture, Arabic 13–14, 18

Damascus 56, 90, 92
Damour 74
Death of a Princess 103
divorce 30, 31
Doha 113, 114
Druze 46, 52, 59–62
Dubai 98, 106, 107

Eden, Sir Anthony 39, 40
Egypt 33–44; British rule
  37–8; economy 35, 39, 40,
  43–4; history 36–42;
  independence 37; law 16,
  31; peace treaty with

Egypt – *contd*
  Israel 20, 41–3, 95, 138;
  population 33–5; Second
  World War 37–8
European Economic
  Community (EEC) 130

Fairouz 18
Faisal, Amir 82
Farouk, King 38
Fateh 71–4, 76
Fez 129, iii, xvi
First World War 15, 37, 46,
  82
France 46, 90, 131–2
Franjieh, Suleiman 63, 65
French North Africa 7
Front de Libération
  Nationale (FLN) 131–2
fundamentalism, Islamic 7,
  31, 44, 55, 62–3, 102, 145

Gaza strip 42, 76
Geagea, Dr Samir 64–5
Gemayal, President Amin
  50–2, 55, 56, 65
Gemayel, President Bashir
  75
Glubb Pasha 39, 83, 84
Golan Heights 93
Gordon, General 145
Gulf Co-operation Council
  (GCC) 104–5, 114
Gulf States 97–114, 115; *see
  also under names of states*
Gulf War 20, 95, 105, 107,
  115–23, 104, 117; causes 115–18;
  effect on Gulf States 109,
  111; mediation attempts
  119–20

Hajj 26
Hassan II, King 126, 128, 131
Hizbollah 50, 61–3
Hobeika, Elie 56, 57, 61, 62,
  65
Hormuz, Straights of 105,
  109, 120
Hussein, King 19, 81, ii;
  accession 83; dismisses
  Glubb Pasha 84; expels
  PLO 72, 85–6;

Hussein, King – *contd*
marriages 89; relations
with PLO 85–7; seeks
peace settlement with
PLO 80, 87–8, 93
Hussein, President Saddam
95, 116, 118, 120, 123

Ibn Saud 101, 103
Industrial Revolution 15, 30
Iran 63, 115–23; revolution
31, 104, 118, 119, *see also*
Gulf War
Iraq 104, 105, 115–23; oil
reserves 123; secrecy 121
Islam 22–32; birth 11, 14,
22–4, 124; expansion 24–5;
five pillars 25; practices
27; prayer 25; revival 18,
32; split 28–9, 60
Islamic Amal 61, 63
Islamic Council 31
Islamic Jihad 57, 109
Ismail, Abdel-Fatah 147–8
Ismailis 29
Israel: boundaries 19, 70;
creation 19, 68, 70, 82;
invasion of Lebanon
49–50, 55, 61, 67, 73, 74;
peace treaty with Egypt
20, 41–3, 95, 138; US
support 19, 87;
withdrawal from
Lebanon 52

Jeddah 25, 99, 100
Jerash 85, 89
Jerusalem 11, 69–71, 79, 85,
86
jihad 31, 118
Jordan 81–9; creation 81–3;
economy 85, 86 in Six Day
War 85; in Arab–Israeli
War 86; re-establishes
diplomatic ties with
Egypt 43
Judaism 23, 24
Jumblatt, Walid 62, 66

Ka'aba 22–3, 25, 26
Karami, Rashid 65
Kharg Island 111, 120
Khartoum 144, 145
Khomeni, Ayatollah 61,
117, xiv
Khoramshahr 119
Kissinger, Henry 91
Koran 6, 23–6, 29, 141, xiv
Kurds 116, 117

Kuwait 57, 97, 104, 109–10

law 16, 29–31
Lawrence of Arabia 11, 81–3
Lebanese Communist Party
63
Lebanese Forces militia 52,
61, 64, 65
Lebanon 10, 11, 45–66; civil
war 7, 73–6; communities
16, 31, 59–60; creation 46;
French influence 46;
history 46–8; Israeli
intervention 7, 49–50, 55,
61, 67, 73; National Pact
47, 59, 60; organisations
60–2; Syrian intervention
49; US involvement 51; *see
also* Beirut
Libya 61, 138–43; American
raids 57, 142–3; economy
143; independence 139;
Italian rule 138; People's
Bureaux 141–2; relations
with Arab states 140–1

Maghreb 7, 125–43; *see also
under names of countries*
Mahdi, Sadiq el 145–6
Manama 111, 112
Marada 63, 65
Maronites 46, 59–65
Mauritania 126–7
Mecca 11, 22–6, 99, 102
Mohammed, Ali Nasser
147–8
Morocco 124, 126, 127–30;
economy 129–30; history
128; Jewish community
128, 131
Mouvement de la Tendance
Islamique (MTI) 136
Movement on Non-Aligned
Nations 133
Mubarak, President Hosni
31, 42–4, vii
Muhammad, Prophet 23–5,
27, 99, 128; sayings 30
Multi-National Force (MNF)
50, 53, 54, 65
Murabitoun 62, xi
music 18–19
Muslim Brotherhood 38, 92
Mzali, Mohamed 137

Nasser, President Gamal
Abdel vii: becomes
President 38; nationalises
Suez Canal 39–40;

Nasser, President Gamal
Abdel – *contd*
humiliated by Six Day
War 20, 40; death 40;
nationalism 8, 32, 71, 84,
140; socialism 44
nationalism, Arab 7, 8, 83,
84, 91, 140
National Liberal Party
(NLP) 62
Neguib, General
Muhammed 38
Neo-Destour party 134
Nile, River 34, 145, v
Nimeri, President Gaffar
144–5
North Yemen 148–9

oil: boom 97, 98, 110, 113, i;
price reductions 35, 130,
134; price rises in
mid-1970s 9–10, 20, 129
Oman 97, 104, 107–9, xiii
Organisation de l'Armée
Secrète (OAS) 132
Organisation of African
Unity 127, 141
Organisation of Petroleum
Exporting Countries
(OPEC) 108, 116
Ottoman Empire 6, 15, 36,
46, 82, 116

Palestine 6, 67–70; British
mandate 68–70;
partitioning 70
Palestine Liberation
Organisation (PLO) 20;
creation 72, 85; expelled
from Jordan 48, 72, 85–6;
in Lebanon 48–50, 63–4,
72–6, xi; withdrawal from
Beirut 67, 75–6, 78, 139;
split 78, 95
Palestinians 67–80; refugees
70, 71, 78–9, 85; *see also*
Palestine Liberation
Organisation
pan-Arabism 19–29, 38, 40,
48, 71, 140
Peres, Shimon 43, 131
Phalange Party 61, 62, 64, 65
pilgrimage 25, 99
poetry 14, 18
Polisario 126–7, 140
Popular Liberation Army 64
Port Said 33, 38, 40
Progressive Socialist Party
(PSP) 61, 62, 66

Qabous, Sultan 108, 109
Qadafi, Colonel 78, 138–43, xvi
Qatar 97, 104, 113–14
Quethoum, Umm 18, 89

Rabat 86, 127, 130
Rabin, Yitzhak 55
Ramadan 25, 27, 98, 112
Ras al-Khaimah 106, 107
Reagan, President Ronald 138, 143
Riyadh 98, 99, 101, 105, iv

Sabra refugee camp 50, 75–6, ix
Sadat, President Anwar: becomes President 40; amends divorce laws 31; attacks Israelis in Sinai 41; economic policy 41, 43, 44; peace treaty with Israel 33, 41–2, 104, 138, xvi; assassination 42, vii
Saharan Arab Democratic Republic 127
Saudi-Arabia 83, 97–104; foreign workers 98, 100, 101; oil revenues 100, 101, 104; regional policy 103–4; size 10, 97; society 102–3; women 18, 28, 101, 102
scholarship 14, 27, 29–31
Second World War 11, 37–8, 69, 138
Shah of Iran 31, 104, 116–18
Sharia'a 8, 29, 145
Sharjah 106, 107
Shatt al-Arab waterway 116, 117, 123, xiv
Shiia 28–9, 60

Shiites; in Iran 123; in Iraq 118; in Lebanon 47, 54, 55, 60
Sinai 11, 35, 40, 41
Six Day War (1967) 20, 32, 40, 41, 71, 140
South Lebanon Army 64
Soviet Union 40, 94, 104, 123, 141, 147, 149
Spain 14, 24, 126
Sudan 144–6
Sudanese People's Liberation Movement (SPLM) 145, 146
Suez Canal 11, 33, 41; building 36–7; nationalisation 39; revenues 43
Suez War (1956) 7, 39–40, 89
Sunnis 28–9, 60; in Lebanon 47, 60, 62; in Morocco 128; in Syria 91
Sykes-Picot agreement 82
Syria 89–96: Arab–Israeli war 93; economy 95–6; history 89–91; intervention in Lebanon 49, 54, 56, 63, 73, 93; merger with Egypt 40, 91; Six Day War 93; support for PLO dissidents 76
Syrian Socialist National Party (SSNP) 63

Tehran 95, 124, 133
Tel al-Zaatar 74
terrorism 6, 43, 72, 73, 142; causes 9, 79; hijacking 133, 142
tourism 43, 134, 136
Transjordan 82–3
Tripoli (Lebanon) 67, 76, 90, v

Tripoli (Libya) 138, 139, 142, 148, xv, xvi
Tunis 42, 80, 135, 137, 138
Tunisia 124–6, 134–8; economy 136; independence 134

United Arab Emirates (UAE) 97, 104, 106–7, xii, xiii
United Arab Republic 40, 91
United Nations Interim Force (UNIFIL) 50, 63, 74
United Nations Resolution 242 80, 87
United States: Beirut embassy 51, 94, xi; involvement in Lebanon 51–3, 94; raids on Libya 57, 142–3, xv; Sixth Fleet 53, 142; support for Israel 19, 87; support for Iraq 122
Utopianism, Islamic 7–8

Voice of the Arabs radio station 38, 84

Waite, Terry 57
Wazzan, Chafic 52, 54, 55, 62
West Bank 41, 70, 76, 78, 82, 85
Western Sahara dispute 126
women, in Arab world: clothing 15–16, 22, 26, 28, 101, 136–7, i; education 16, 18; freedom 16, 18; status 15, 23, 27–8, 136; work 18

Zionism 19, 69, 70